Pants fit for your figure

point-by-point pattern adjustment

Louise Bame

Cover design by Jeanne R. Hurst

Illustrations by Jeanne R. Hurst and Marcia Moir

Pattern diagrams by Michael Bame

Copyright©1978 Louise Bame

Second printing, 1979

Published by Vista Publications
3010 Santa Monica Boulevard, Suite 221
Santa Monica, California 90404

Printed in the United States of America
Library of Congress Catalog Card Number 78-63390
ISBN 0-932740-00-6

To my students, past, present, and future, and to women everywhere who want to make pants with perfect fit, even for imperfect figures.

My thanks to all who gave me encouragement and assistance in writing this book. I am grateful to the many students and friends who participated in various stages of the development of the method and to all who offered suggestions about the writing.

Valuable input was given by several people from the viewpoint of the consumer. Special recognition goes to Josephine Carreno, Thelma Norwood, Camelia O'Connor, and Fran Schneider, for their generous contribution of many hours of conscientious testing and review, and for faithful support when I needed it the most.

I feel very lucky to have the artistry of Jeanne Hurst for the cover design. My thanks to her and to Marcia Moir for their combined efforts in producing the illustrations.

I am deeply grateful to Helen Crocker for her sensitive and perceptive editing, and for kindness beyond measure.

I thank my husband, Bill, and sons, Michael and Richard, who helped in countless ways, the most visible of which are the pattern diagrams which Michael prepared so exactly. Without the interest, understanding, and cooperation of my family and friends it would not have been possible to complete this book.

Louise Bame

Contents

People, Patterns, and Fit

If people were made like paper dolls, the same pattern would fit everyone. But people are individuals. Standard sizes do not fit all figures. If you compared yourself to a dozen other people who have the same waist and hip measurements as you do, not one would have a shape identical to yours, yet all would buy the same size pattern. Of course, they will not all get the same fit.

Pattern Size and Body Measurements

Pants patterns are sold by size according to body measurement of waist and hip circumference. These are only two of the measurements that go into the making of the pattern. Unless your figure is the same as or very close to the standard of the pattern company in all respects, you are bound to need some adjustments to make the finished garment fit you.

Even if your figure is ideal you may have a longer or shorter crotch depth or leg length than the standard. The pattern must be adjusted for these *before* cutting. If your waist and hip circumferences are not exactly the same as those specified, the pattern must be adjusted for these also.

Ease Allowance and Personal Preference

The *ease allowance* is the extra amount included in the pattern to provide room for comfort and movement. The amount of ease varies with each designer and is *not* the same for every pattern of a given size. Some people like a looser fit and some a snugger fit. The amount of ease that suits *your* personal preference may be different than the amount provided in the pattern.

THE MINIMUM ADJUSTMENTS

Because of the variability of pattern proportions, body proportions, and personal preferences for ease, every pattern should be checked and adjusted for the major lengths and widths. These are the minimum adjustments:

1. Crotch depth
2. Length from waist to hem
3. Width at the hipline
4. Width at the waistline

THE SPECIAL ADJUSTMENTS

If you have either a flat or a prominent seat or a high tummy bulge, you will need some additional adjustments. Other figure variations that need special attention include high hip bulge, thigh bulges, knock-knees, and uneven figures with one high hip or one wide thigh. These characteristics are not at all unusual, but it is unrealistic to expect any commercial pattern to accommodate all of these variations.

It is possible to predict closely the pattern requirements to fit these figure variables. A special right angle measurement of *waist indentation* makes it possible to predict your pattern requirements closer than ever before. By making these adjustments on the pattern *before cutting* you can save a lot of trial and error re-fitting afterwards.

Compare your figure shape to the illustrations in CHART B. If you have any of these figure characteristics, you may make additional adjustments that apply to you. These special adjustments are:

1. Waist depth
2. Wedge
3. Crotch point extension
4. Inseam
5. Crotch curve
6. Side seam curve

PRE-FIT PATTERNS AND THE PERSONAL MASTER PATTERN

You can avoid going through time-consuming adjustment and fitting procedures every time you sew by learning to *pre-fit* your patterns. By determining your fitting requirements in a simple basic style, you can make a *personal master pattern* to use again and again with a variety of fashion patterns of many styles. Making a personal master pattern involves the following steps:

1. Measure your figure.
2. Select pattern and fabric.
3. Adjust the pattern to requirements.
4. Make pants to test the pattern.
5. Evaluate the fit and make corrections.
6. Make a durable copy of the final pattern.

Each step is explained in detail in the following pages. Please familiarize yourself with the contents of the entire book before you start work on your pattern. Assemble the tools and supplies - a checklist is provided in the appendix. Then follow all of the directions. At the end of each step, review the instructions and check that you did everything correctly before going on to the next step.

"We all wear size 12"

Taking Body Measurements

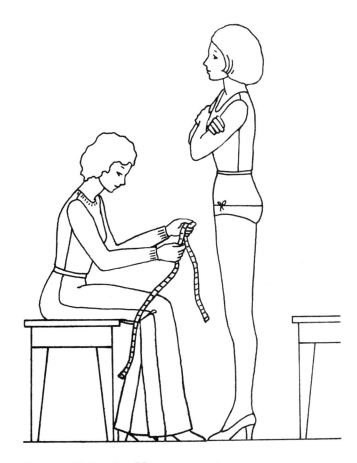

What to Wear

Your measurements should be taken over only the undergarments you usually wear with pants. If you usually wear a girdle, wear one when you are measured. Be sure the top of your girdle and the top of your panties or pantyhose are in the proper position at your natural waistline.

Mark your waist with a narrow belt fastened as snugly as you would like a waistband to fit. Sit down and be sure it feels comfortable. At the same time, be sure it is snug enough to stay in place without shifting while you are being measured. The bottom of the belt should be exactly at your natural waistline. This is where your body creases when you bend forward and from side to side. If you don't have a narrow belt, fasten a firm tape measure around your waist.

Mark your hipline by tying a piece of 1/8" elastic at seat level. This is at the most extended part of the buttocks. The elastic should be level with the floor. Leave your shoes on so your posture will be natural.

How to Stand

Stand comfortably erect with your arms folded over your chest so they are out of the way, or you may hold this book while you record the measurements. Assume a natural stance with your weight equally balanced on both feet. Your legs should be neither farther apart nor closer together than you normally stand. Take a deep breath, exhale, then stay still and let the measurement taker do the looking and the moving.

How to Take the Measurements

You will need help to get accurate body measurements. The person taking the measurements should be seated. Place a chair on each side of the person being measured so the measurement taker can change position easily. *It is important that the person being measured doesn't keep changing posture.*

Use a new tape measure of non-stretch fiberglass. Take the measurements amply. Hold the tape measure just snug enough that it does not fall slack. Be sure not to compress the flesh or you may get an overly tight reading.

Record the measurements on CHART A: PERSONAL DATA FOR PANTS. Throughout this book the items on CHART A are referred to as "A-1, A-2", etc.

CHART A: PERSONAL DATA FOR PANTS

Body Measurements

Floor to Waist:

1. Center front . . . . _____

2. Center back . . . . _____

3. Right side . . . . _____

4. Left side . . . . _____

Waist Indentation:

5. Center front . . . . _____

6. Center back . . . . _____

Circumferences:

7. Waist . . . . _____

8. High hip . . . . _____
   (3" below waist)

9. Full hip . . . . _____
   (seat level)

Lengths: [on high side]

10. Hip depth . . . . _____
    (waist to hipline)

11. Waist to middle of knee . . . . _____

12. Side length . . . . _____
    (waist to sole of foot, or as desired)

13. Crotch depth . . . . _____
    (waist to table top)

Observations

14. Special figure characteristics

    (List)

4

CHART B: SPECIAL FIGURE CHARACTERISTICS

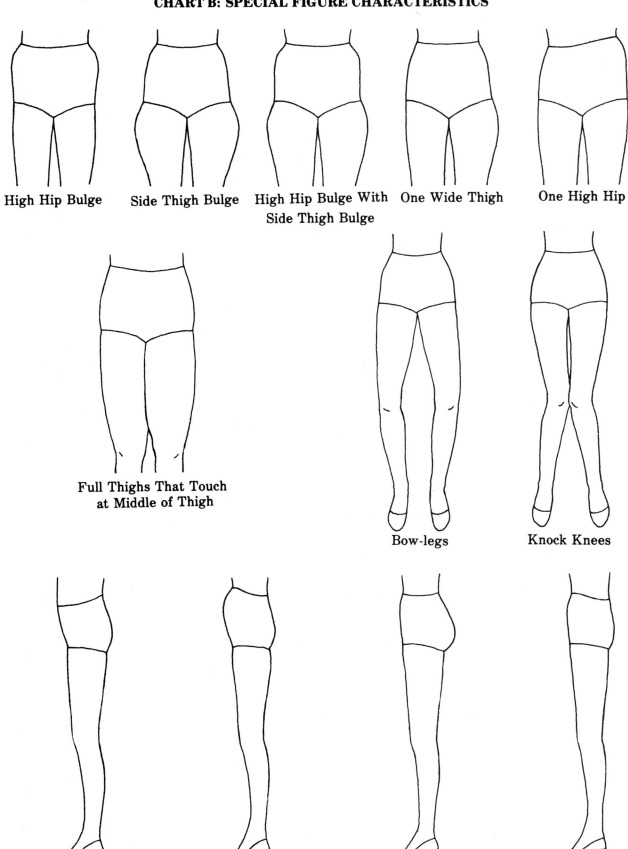

High Hip Bulge

Side Thigh Bulge

High Hip Bulge With
Side Thigh Bulge

One Wide Thigh

One High Hip

Full Thighs That Touch
at Middle of Thigh

Bow-legs

Knock Knees

Waistline Dips Low
in Front

Waistline Dips Low in Back
High Tummy Bulge

Prominent Seat

Flat Seat

BODY MEASUREMENTS

Floor-To-Waist Measurements

The comparison of the four floor-to-waist measurements shows where your waistline dips or rises and how much. To measure this easily, anchor your tape measure to a yardstick with tacks or tape. Fasten the zero end face down against the zero end of the yardstick. Fasten again at the 27" mark.

A-1 to A-4: Center Front, Center Back, Left Side, and Right Side

Hold the yardstick upright with the zero end touching the floor. Hold the side with the stick toward you so that the tape measure is against the body of the person being measured. Let the tape measure follow the body curve to the waistline.

Record the measurement from the floor to the *bottom* of the belt at center front, center back, and the center of each side. If one side is higher than the other, the high side is to be circled on Chart A.

Waist Indentation

This is the horizontal distance from the waist to a flat surface held vertically against the body at the tummy or hipline. It eliminates guesswork in evaluating the degree of prominence of the seat and tummy.

For the flat surface you may use a board or any convenient object that is rigid. A piece of plywood or masonite about 9" x 12" is fine, or a hard-cover book. Use a dressmaker's gauge to take the measurement.

A-5: Center Front

Hold the board lightly against the tummy and be sure to keep it vertical. Hold the gauge horizontally so the zero end touches the bottom of the belt at center front with the other end at the top of the board. Record the distance from the belt to the board.

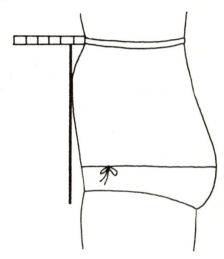

A-6: Center Back

Hold the board lightly against the seat, keeping it vertical. Hold the gauge horizontally so the zero end touches the bottom of the belt at center back with the other end at the top of the board. Take care not to press the gauge into the hollow of the spine. Record the distance from the belt to the board.

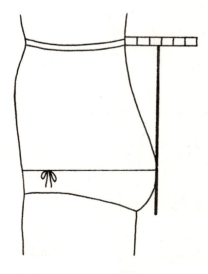

Circumferences:

A-7: Waist

Delay taking this measurement until the others have been completed, in order not to disturb the position of the belt that marks the waist.

When you are ready to measure the waist, remove the belt and hold the tape measure around the waist to the same degree of snugness. Remember, this measurement should be the way you want your waistband to fit.

A-8: High Hip

Measure down 3" from the bottom of the belt on the high side and take the high hip circumference at this level. Keep the tape measure parallel to the floor.

A-9: Full Hip

Measure the circumference at the hipline marker with the tape measure parallel to the floor.

Lengths:

Take all the lengths from the center of the side. If the right and left sides of the body are different, measure from the *high* side, since the pattern is adjusted for the high side.

A-10: Hip Depth

Measure from the bottom of the belt to the hipline marker.

A-11: Waist to Middle of Knee

Measure from the bottom of the belt to the middle of the knee. This is even with the crease that forms at the back of the knee when the knee is bent.

A-12: Side Length of Pants

Measure from the bottom of the belt to the sole of the foot, or to the desired finished length.

A-13: Crotch Depth

The person being measured should sit on a flat bench or table top, very erect, arms folded, without leaning to either side. Measure from the bottom of the belt to the table top. Take care to locate the *center* of the side. Follow the body curve from waist to hipline, then straight to the table.

Now go back to A-7 and record the waist measurement.

OBSERVATIONS

A-14: Special Figure Characteristics

Study your figure in a full-length mirror and compare to the illustrations in Chart B. Record any special characteristics that apply to you.

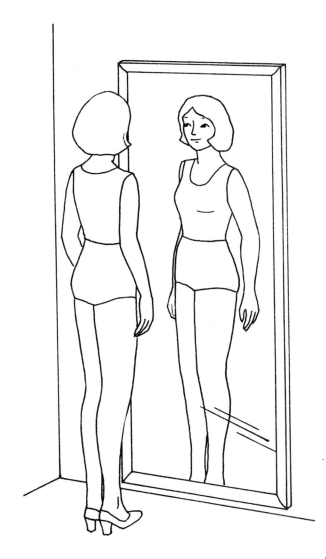

Selecting Pattern and Fabric

THE BASIC PATTERN

Choose a simple basic pants pattern with straight legs and two side seams. It may have darts and a waistband or it may have a waistline casing with elastic or a drawstring. A waistband should be at the natural waistline.

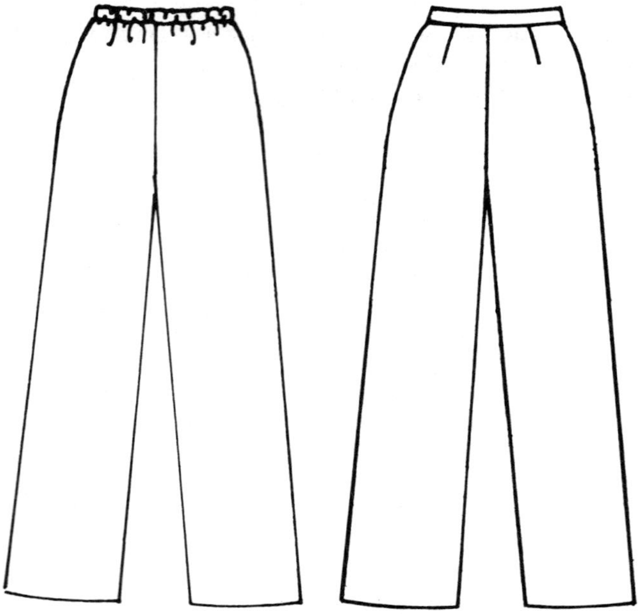

It is easier to *test* your fit in pants with an elastic waist than in pants with darts and a waistband. Wait until later for hip huggers, hip yokes, cut-in pockets, and curved seaming. Such extra style details complicate the procedure of determining your essential fitting requirements.

Read the description printed on the back of the pattern envelope. It will usually tell if the waistline is lowered and if the legs are flared, straight, or tapered. Also, study the sketch of the pattern shape. The width of each pantleg at the bottom edge is usually listed for each size.

MISSES' PANTS

Straight-legged pants. View A has waistband and back zipper closing. View B has elasticized waistline.

BODY MEASUREMENTS					
Waist Size	24	25	26 1/2	28	30
Hip	33 1/2	34 1/2	36	38	40
PANTS A					
44/45" */**	2 3/8	2 5/8	2 5/8	2 5/8	2 3/4
54" *	1 5/8	1 3/4	1 3/4	2 3/8	2 3/8
PANTS B					
44/45" */**	2 3/8	2 3/8	2 5/8	2 5/8	2 3/4
54" *	1 5/8	1 3/4	1 3/4	1 7/8	2 3/8
INTERFACING A					
18,21,25" Fusible	7/8	7/8	7/8	1	1
36" Non-Woven	1/8	1/8	1/8	1/8	1/8

Obvious diagonal fabrics are not suitable. For one-way design: use nap yardage and nap layout. Allowance for matching plaid and stripes not included in yardages given.

* with nap, shading, pile or one-way design.
** without nap, shading or pile or with a two-way design.

Width at lower edge					
Pants A,B (each leg)	19 1/2	20	20 3/4	21 3/4	22 3/4
Finished side length from waist					
Pants A,B	41 3/4	42	42 1/4	42 1/2	42 3/4

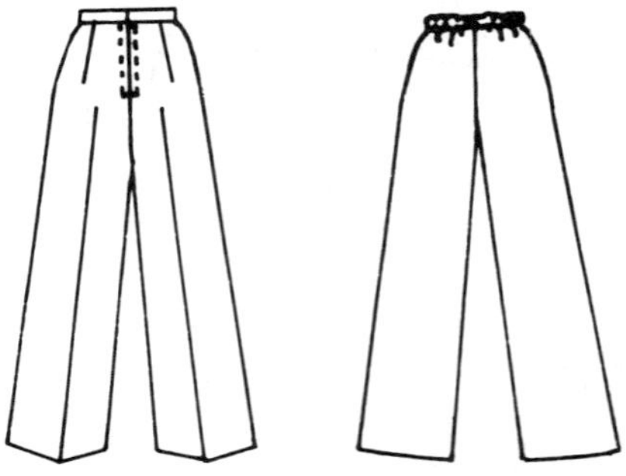

A B

Measure around the bottom of a pair of pants in your wardrobe or in a store for comparison. Buy a pattern that has a pant-leg width close to the width you like.

Pattern Size

Select the pattern size according to your full hip circumference. If your hip measurement is between sizes, buy the larger size. A one-size pattern is easier to work with than most multi-sized patterns.

Fabric

Either woven or knit fabric may be used, but select a weight comparable to what you would normally use for your wardrobe. Polyester and cotton broadcloth is best for testing. Lighter weight fabric, such as gingham, may not give a reliable test. Delay using heavy or crisp fabrics, such as corduroy or gabardine, until you have completed your master pattern.

If you prefer knits, test the pattern in a firm double-knit of polyester, wool, or a blend. Don't try to test your basic fit in jersey or cotton knit. Jersey is too thin and flexible and cotton knit is too soft and does not hold its shape well enough. The same thing applies to acrylic. Read the label on the bolt before you buy so you will know what you are getting.

Select a light or medium solid color. A *woven* check or stripe may be used if the colors are soft. It is hard to see the markings on dark colors, strong color contrasts and prints.

Yardage Requirements

For testing buy a little extra fabric to allow for ample seams and hems: in fabric 45" wide, get two times your side length (A-12) plus 12"; in fabric 58" wide, get one side length plus 12" in sizes up to 38" hip. If your hip measures more than 38" you will probably need two times your side length plus 12".

Select a firm "no-roll" elastic in either 3/4" or 1" width. Polyester elastic is usually more durable and will shrink less than a rayon elastic. Since the shrinkage is unpredictable, buy 6" more than your waist measure.

Preparation

If your fabric is washable, wash it to pre-shrink and soften it before you cut out your pants. Press if needed. If the label states "Dryclean only", play safe and have your dry-cleaner pre-shrink the fabric before you cut. Be sure to wash the elastic before you measure and cut.

Understanding the Pattern

Pattern Terms

Before you set to work to adjust your pattern let's be sure we understand one another with regard to the use of certain terms and procedures. In this book the same terms are used in pattern adjustment as in my system of pattern drafting. These will be easier to understand if you know something about how a pattern is made.

The explanation that follows will make more sense as you actually work with your pattern. It is presented here to familiarize you with terms and concepts that you may not know. Although you are eager to get started with your pattern, taking the time to go over this now may save you from wasting time on needless errors later.

THE POINT-BY-POINT SYSTEM

The basis of the Point-By-Point system of pattern adjustment is the identification of pattern points by number. A pants pattern is drafted to specific measurements at twelve points. These are designated in order, starting at the top, center, and proceeding counterclockwise around the front pattern, clockwise around the back pattern. This makes it easy for you to find your place at any time.

THE PATTERN POINTS

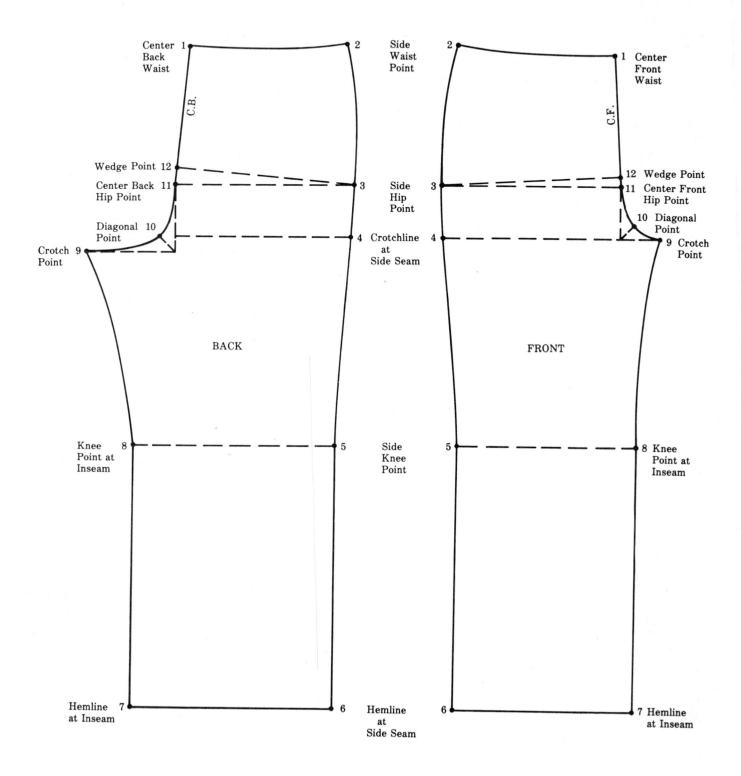

Center 1 Back Waist

2 Side Waist Point

2 Center Front Waist 1

C.B.

C.F.

Wedge Point 12

Center Back 11 Hip Point

3 Side Hip Point

3 12 Wedge Point

11 Center Front Hip Point

Diagonal 10 Point

10 Diagonal Point

Crotch 9 Point

4 Crotchline at Side Seam

4 9 Crotch Point

BACK

FRONT

Knee 8 Point at Inseam

5 Side Knee Point

5 8 Knee Point at Inseam

Hemline 7 at Inseam

6 Hemline at Side Seam

6 7 Hemline at Inseam

10

THE MAKING OF A PATTERN

First an ease allowance is added to the body measurements of waist circumference, hip circumference, and crotch depth. The circumferences are divided into front and back sections. Each front and back measurement is divided in half, since the pattern is made for the right half of the body. Dimensions vary with size and figure proportions. Exact amounts are not given here.

The pattern is drafted without seam allowance or hem allowance. These are added after all the seamlines have been drawn.

Guide Lines

The pattern starts with guide lines drawn to form a rectangle. The four corners are labeled A, B, C, and D. Line AD becomes the *center front* (C.F.) or *center back* (C.B.). The width of the rectangle represents the *hipline* (H.L.). This is approximately one-fourth of the body measurement at the hipline, including ease. The length represents the *hip depth*, which is the distance from the waist to the hipline.

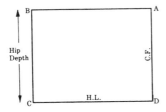

The average *waistline* (W.) dips at the center back and at the center front, although on some people the waistline rises at center front. The amount the waistline dips or rises at the center in relation to the side is called *waist depth*.

Here is a waistline that dips.

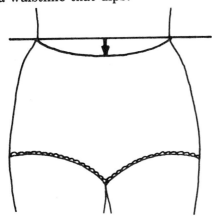

The waist depth is marked DOWN from A at Pt. 1.

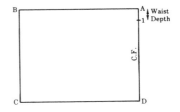

Here is a waistline that rises.

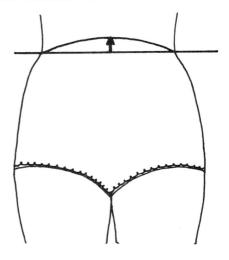

The waist depth is marked UP from A at Pt. 1.

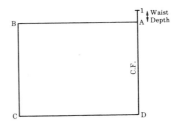

The *side waist point* (S.W. Pt.) is marked IN from B at Pt. 2. The waistline curve is drawn from Pt. 1 to Pt. 2. Darts are added for a fitted waistline. They are omitted when a casing and elastic are used.

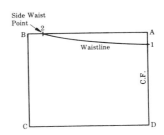

The *side hip point* (S.H. Pt.) is Pt. 3. This is the same as C. This is where the hipline meets the *side seamline* (S.S.). The *side hip curve* is drawn from Pt. 2 to Pt. 3. This is the beginning of the side seamline.

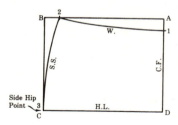

THE HIP BLOCK

This much of the pattern, from waist to hipline, is called the *hip block*. It serves as the beginning of both skirt and pants patterns.

Pantlegs

For pants, the two vertical lines of the rectangle are extended downward from the hip block to the desired pants length. These are the *side line* (S.L.) and the *center line* (C.L.).

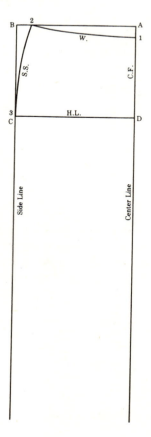

The *crotchline* (Cr.L.), *kneeline* (K.L.), and *hemline* (Hem.) are drawn at right angles to the vertical guide lines.

The *crotch depth* is the length from waist to crotchline at Pt. 4. This is drawn to body measurement including ease. The *kneeline* marks the length from waist to knee. The *hemline* marks the finished side length of the pants from waist to hem.

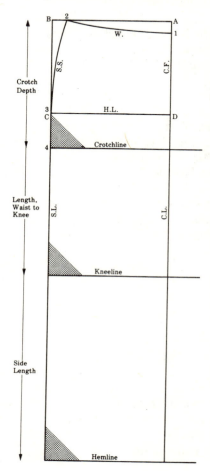

The side seamline is curved inward from the crotch-line at Pt. 4 to the *side knee point* (S.K. Pt.) at Pt. 5. It is drawn straight from Pt. 5 to the hemline at side seam (Hem. at S.S.) which is Pt. 6. This completes the side seamline.

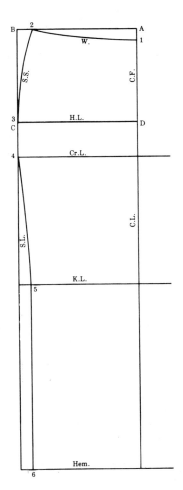

The *inseam* (Ins.) is the seamline on the inner side of the leg. It is drawn straight from the *hemline at inseam* (Hem. at Ins.), Pt. 7, to the *knee point at inseam* (K. Pt. at Ins.), Pt. 8. It is curved from Pt. 8 to the *crotch point* (Cr. Pt.), Pt. 9. The crotch point is where the crotch seam meets the inseam.

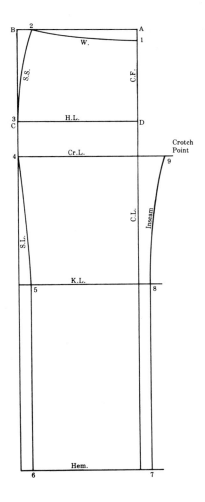

The amount the crotchline is extended beyond the center line to the crotch point is called the *crotch point extension*. This amount is approximately one-fourth the hipline width of the front pattern and one-half the hipline width of the back pattern.

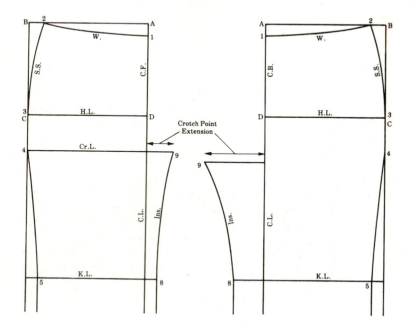

The Crotch Curve

The depth of the crotch curve is marked on a diagonal guide line at Pt. 10, the *diagonal point* (Diag. Pt.). The crotch curve is then drawn from Pt. 9 through Pt. 10 to Pt. 11, the *center front hip point* (C.F. Hip Pt.) and *center back hip point* (C.B. Hip Pt.). Pt. 11 is the same as D.

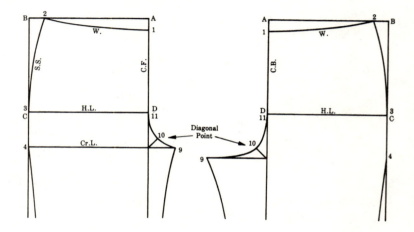

The crotch curve is made lower in back than in front because the body curves lower under the seat than under the abdomen. The back inseam is purposely made shorter than the front inseam, but is stretched to match when sewing. This reduces clinging under the seat.

The Wedge

One more step provides extra length at the center seam without changing the side seam length. The hip block is tilted to add a *wedge* which gives extra ease for sitting. This is done by cutting the pattern along the hipline and spreading the pattern pieces apart. The amount of wedge is marked upward from Pt. 11 at Pt. 12, the *wedge point* (We. Pt.). The line connecting the wedge point to the side hip point is called the *wedge line*. The *wedge* is the space between the hipline and the wedge line.

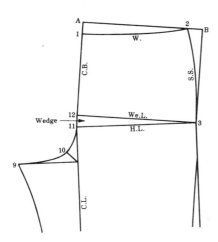

Some designers omit the wedge in front but there is always a wedge in back.

The back pattern is the same as the front except for the darts, the wedge, the back crotch curve, and the inseam position. The waistline darts are longer and wider in back than in front. The back wedge is larger than in front. The back crotch curve is lower and wider to extend farther under the seat. The inseam is farther from the center line making the pants leg wider in back.

The guide lines are omitted from the final copy of the pattern. Seam and hem allowance are added, and either a waistband, a casing, or a facing to finish the waistline. The stitching lines (sewing lines) are shown as broken lines and the cutting lines as solid lines. The grainline (straight-of-goods) is drawn parallel to the center line.

By now you may feel that all this is more than you really wanted to know about pants. Don't worry, you don't have to remember all these details. All you need to know for the moment is that the information is here. Any time you come to a term you can't remember you will know where to look for it.

Now let's take a coffee break before we continue.

Adjusting the Pattern

PRELIMINARIES

Press the pattern with a warm, dry iron to smooth out the creases. It makes your work a lot easier to stabilize the tissue pattern by ironing it onto plastic coated freezer paper. Have your iron warm, not hot. Unless it is Teflon, protect the surface of your iron by holding a sheet of plain tissue paper under the soleplate so it won't come in contact with the plastic. Work from the center toward the edges of each pattern piece so you won't trap air bubbles in the middle. Do not trim the excess paper around the pattern.

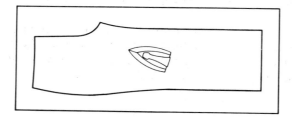

The stabilized copy of the original pattern will be used as a tracing guide when you need to alter curved seamlines during the process of adjustment. This procedure preserves the shape of the original pattern curves as closely as possible.

Label each pattern point as shown in the diagram, THE PATTERN POINTS.

Use a yardstick to extend the *grainline* (Gr. L.) on front and back patterns to within 1" of the waistline and hemline. Draw the *crotchline* on the *front* pattern, in blue, from Pt. 9 to the side seamline, at right angles to the grainline. Label Cr. L.

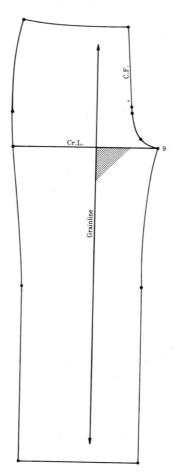

To draw a line at right angles to any other line, use a triangle, an L-square, or a piece of cardboard with square corner. It is easier to be accurate if each edge of the triangle or square is about 12" long. Right angles are indicated in this book by a shaded triangle.

Using different colors of pencil for lines that serve different purposes helps save confusion. The original pattern lines are traced in black #2 lead pencil. Use blue pencil for guide lines, hipline, crotchline, and kneeline. After your adjustments are marked, use red pencil for the *adjusted* stitching lines, hemlines, and the fold line of the casing. Keep your pencils sharp for accuracy.

Trace the *adjustment line* (Adj. L.) printed a few inches above the crotch on front and back patterns. It is usually a double line labelled "Lengthen or Shorten Here". Omit all other adjustment lines. If there is no adjustment line printed on your pattern, draw your own 2½" above the crotch points on front and back patterns, at right angles to the grainline.

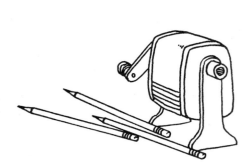

Make a *working copy* of the pattern on semi-transparent pattern paper, *omitting* the cutting lines. You are much less apt to make an error when you see only the stitching lines and grain lines.

Pattern paper can be purchased at fabric stores, or you can use unglazed shelf paper. Lay the pattern paper over the pattern and pin the layers together to prevent slipping. If your pattern paper is the kind with dots spaced an inch apart, place it so that the grainline coincides with a row of dots.

If you have a light surface underneath you will be able to see the lines through the pattern paper. Be sure to make your lines heavy enough so that you can see them easily. Use a ruler to help you keep straight lines straight. The most satisfactory kind is made of clear, flexible plastic and has the surface marked with vertical and horizontal lines.

In black pencil, carefully trace the grainlines, stitching lines, hemlines, and the foldline of the casing. Crossmark the tip of each dart. Trace the front crotchline in blue. Omit the back crotchline.

Don't forget to trace the waistband pattern.

Leave the working copy of the pattern untrimmed. Keep patterns wrinkle-free by rolling them up when you put them away. Plastic "oilcloth" makes a good pattern storage roll.

Complete the steps below *in the order listed.* Refer to Chart A for the items designated as A-1, A-2, etc. Refer to the Table of Divisions in the appendix to find the answers where division is called for. The measurements you will apply to your pattern are the ones you write in the boxes.

THE MINIMUM ADJUSTMENTS

1. Crotch Depth

Enter your crotch depth (A-13) . . . . _____

Add ease from the chart below . . . . _____

Total . . . . [____]

Full hip (A-9)	Ease
36" or less	3/4"
36-1/2" to 38"	1"
38-1/2" to 40"	1-1/4"
Over 40"	1-1/2"

Locate Pt. 2 on the *front* pattern. This is where the waist seamline or casing foldline meets the side seamline. Ignore any waistline marks printed on the pattern.

Measure the front pattern from Pt. 2 downward along the side seamline and mark your crotch depth total in blue. This is the total shown in the box above. Use a flexible plastic ruler or hold a tape measure on edge to follow the pattern curve.

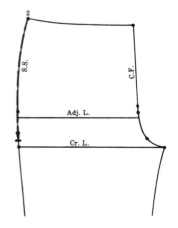

Measure the distance from your mark to the crotchline and record: . . . _____ This is the amount of adjustment. If your mark is below the crotchline, make a "**+**" in front of the amount to indicate an increase. If your mark is above the crotchline, make a "**–**" in front of the amount to indicate a decrease.

To *increase,* cut along the *adjustment line* and spread the pattern pieces apart. Tape a strip of pattern paper underneath one edge. Use "Magic" type transparent tape, the kind you can write on. Mark the amount of increase at each end of the strip and connect with a line. Extend the grainline across the strip. Tape the other pattern edge to the line, matching at the grainline. The cut edges should be exactly parallel.

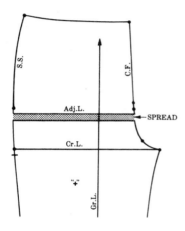

To *decrease,* measure up from the *adjustment line* and mark the amount of decrease at each end. Connect the marks with a parallel line. Cut along the adjustment line and overlap until the two lines meet exactly, matching at the grainline. Tape in place.

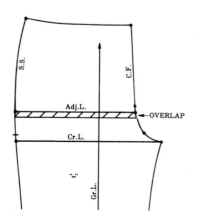

Adjust the crotch depth of the back pattern the *same amount* as you adjusted the front. Cut along the adjustment line and spread or overlap, the same way as on the front pattern.

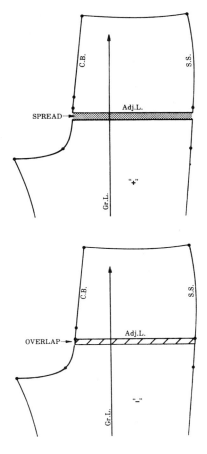

NOTE: Any change in crotch depth must *always* be made the same on front and back.

2. Length, Waist to Hem

Enter your side length (A-12) . . . . □

Measure front pattern from Pt. 2 downward along the side seamline and mark your length in blue. Draw your *hemline* in red from this mark to the inseam, parallel to the original hemline. Label Hem.

Mark your hemline on the back pattern in the same way.

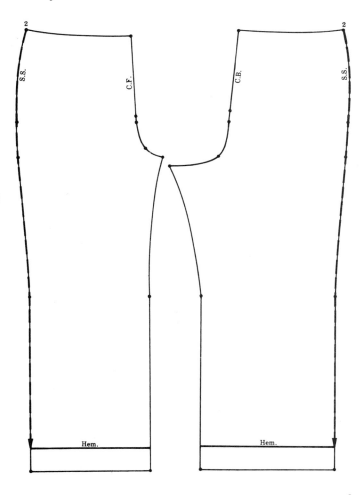

3. Width at Hipline

Enter your hip depth (A-10) . . . .

Measure front pattern from Pt. 2 downward along the side seamline and mark your hip depth in blue. Draw your *hipline* from this mark to the center front seamline, at right angles to the grainline. Label H.L.

Mark your hipline on the back pattern in the same way.

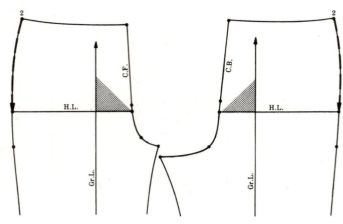

Enter your full hip circumference (A-9) . . . . _____

Add ease from the chart below . . . . _____

Extra ease (See note below) . . . . _____

Total . . . . _____

Divide by 2 . . . .

This is your pattern width at hipline.

Hip (A-9)	Ease	
	Knits	Wovens
Up to 40"	1/2"	1-1/2"
Over 40"	1"	2"

NOTE: *Extra ease is required for people whose high hip measurement is greater than the full hip measurement. If A-9 is greater than A-8, you do not need any extra ease. Enter zero.*

If A-8 is greater than A-9, determine your extra ease as follows:

Enter high hip circumference (A-8) . . . . _____

Enter full hip circumference (A-9) . . . . _____

Find the difference . . . . _____

Divide by 2 . . . . _____

This is your extra ease.

Place the front and back patterns side by side, matching hiplines at the side seamlines. Pin together at Pt. 3. Measure from Pt. 11 at the center back along the hipline toward the center front and mark your total pattern width at hipline in blue.

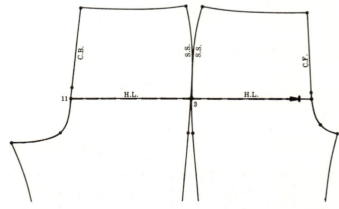

Measure the distance from your mark to Pt. 11 on the center front and record . . . . _____

Divide by 2 . . . .

This is the amount of adjustment for each pattern piece. If your mark is to the right of Pt. 11, make a "+" in front of the amount. If your mark is to the left of Pt. 11, make a "−" in front of the amount.

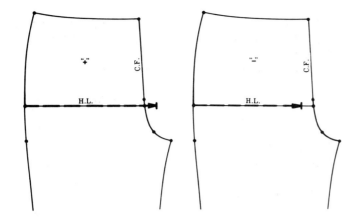

Length, Waist to Knee

Enter your length, waist to knee (A-11) . . . . [ ]

Measure the front pattern from Pt. 2 downward along the side seamline and mark your length, waist to knee, in blue. Draw your *kneeline* from this mark to the inseam, at right angles to the grainline. Label K.L.

Mark your kneeline on the back pattern in the same way.

To *increase* the width at hipline, mark your adjustment OUT from Pt. 3 on front and back patterns in red.

On the back pattern, mark Pt. 4 the same distance below Pt. 3 as on the front pattern. Increase the width at Pt. 4 on front and back patterns by marking OUT the same amount as at Pt. 3. Connect the two marks in red.

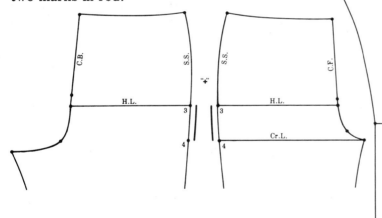

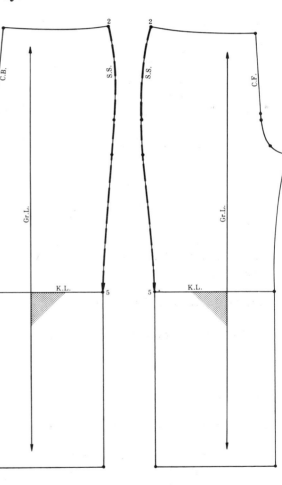

To *decrease* the width at hipline, mark your adjustment IN from Pt. 3 on front and back patterns in red. Mark IN the same amount at Pt. 4. Connect the two marks in red.

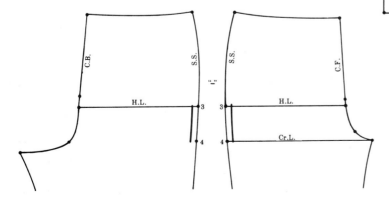

Observe the shape of the side seamlines. If the side seamlines of the pattern you are using are parallel to the grainline below Pt. 4, draw your adjusted side seamlines in red, parallel to the original ones, from your adjusted Pt. 4 to the hemline.

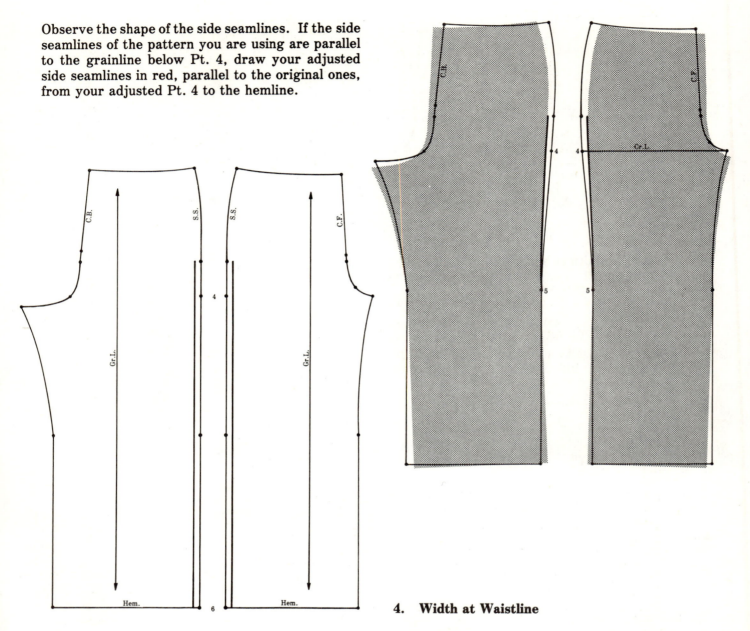

If the side seamlines of the pattern you are using are tapered below Pt. 4, place your front pattern on top of the original pattern front, matching your adjusted Pt. 4 to Pt. 4 of the original with a pin. Using the pin as a pivot point, swing your pattern until it coincides at Pt. 5 with the side seamline of the original pattern. Pin the patterns together in this position and trace the side seamline from the original onto your pattern in red from Pt. 4 to Pt. 5.

Trace the side seamline of the back pattern from Pt. 4 to Pt. 5 in the same way.

4. Width at Waistline

Styles With Casing

Precise fitting at the waist is not necessary when there is a casing gathered with elastic or a drawstring. If any adjustment was made in width at the hipline, mark the *same* adjustment at Pt. 2 on the front and back patterns. Connect the marks from Pt. 2 to Pt. 3 with a red line parallel to the original side seamline.

NOTE: *The waistline must be large enough to pull on over the hips.* The *minimum* width at waistline for woven fabric is half your hip circumference, A-8 or A-9, whichever is larger. It may be ½" less for knits that stretch. Add width at Pt. 2 if needed.

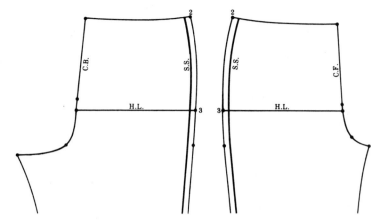

If A-9 is greater than A-8, but the difference is less than 2", enter ½" extra ease. If A-8 is the same as A-9 or greater than A-9, enter ½" extra ease.

Place the front and back patterns side by side, matching waistlines at the side seamlines. Pin together at Pt. 2. Measure from Pt. 1 at the center back along the waistline, skipping darts, and mark your total pattern width at waist from the box above, in blue. Use a flexible ruler or hold a tape measure on edge to follow along the curve accurately.

Styles With Darts

Enter your waist circumference (A-7) . . . . _____

Add ease from the chart below . . . . _____

Extra ease (See NOTE below) . . . . _____

Total . . . . _____

Divide by 2 . . . . [____]

This is the pattern width at waist, *skipping darts.*

Waist (A-7)	Ease	
	Knits	Wovens
Up to 30"	zero	1"
Over 30"	1/2"	1-1/2"

NOTE: *Figures that are padded in the high hip area require additional waistline ease.* Compare your full hip and high hip measurements.

Enter your full hip circumference (A-9) . . . . _____

Enter your high hip circumference (A-8) . . . . _____

Find the difference . . . . _____

If A-9 is greater than A-8 and the difference is 2" or more, no extra ease is needed. Enter zero.

Measure from your mark to Pt. 1 at the center front and record . . . . _____

Divide by 2 . . . . [____]

This is the amount of adjustment for each pattern piece. If your mark is to the right of Pt. 1, make a "+" in front of the amount. If your mark is to the left of Pt. 1, make a "−" in front of the amount.

If the amount of adjustment needed at the waist is the same as or less than at the hipline, make all of the waist adjustment at Pt. 2. If the amount of adjustment at the waist is *more* than at the hipline, make part of the waist adjustment at Pt. 2 and part by changing dart width.

To *increase* the width at the waist, mark your adjustment OUT from Pt. 2 on front and back patterns in red.

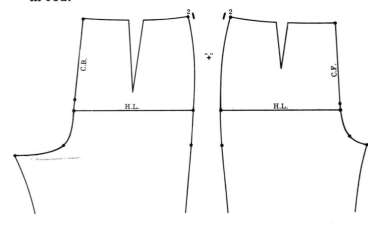

To *decrease* the width at the waist, mark your adjustment IN from Pt. 2 on front and back patterns in red.

To *increase* the waistline, *decrease* the dart width.

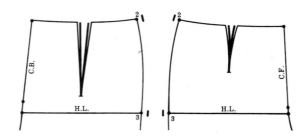

To *decrease* the waistline, *increase* the dart width.

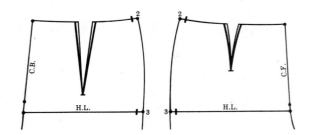

NOTE: After marking the waistline adjustment, measure the resulting waistline from the new marks to make sure it is correct.

All Styles

Place your front pattern on top of the original commercial pattern front, matching your adjusted Pt. 2 to Pt. 2 of the original with a pin. Using the pin as a pivot point, swing your pattern until it coincides at Pt. 3 with the side seamline of the original pattern. Pin the patterns together in this position and trace the side seamline from the original onto your pattern in red from Pt. 2 to Pt. 3.

Trace the side seamline onto the back pattern from Pt. 2 to Pt. 3 in the same way.

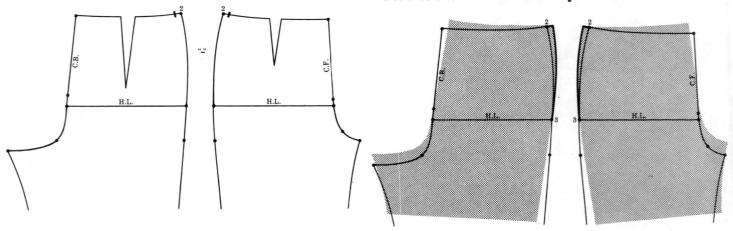

Waistband Length

On the waistband pattern, locate the points where the band meets the placket opening. These points are usually labelled center front, center back, or lap line.

Notice that the waistband pattern is for the whole waistline, rather than for half the body.

Enter your waist circumference (A-7) . . . . □

This is the length your *finished* waistband should be, *not* including underlap or overlap.

Measure from the lap line toward the other end and mark the length you require in red. Re-mark the center halfway between.

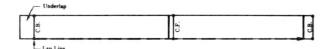

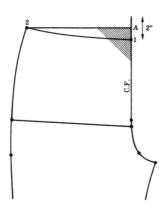

Measure UP or DOWN from Pt. A and mark your *center front waist depth* in blue.

SPECIAL ADJUSTMENTS

5. Waist Depth

Determine the amount your waistline dips or rises at center and compare to the waistline dip of the pattern.

Front

Enter floor-to-waist measure
of your higher side (A-3 or A-4) . . . . ———

Enter floor-to-waist measure
of center front (A-1) . . . . ———

Find the difference . . . . □

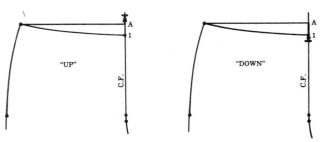

Place your front pattern over the original pattern matching your adjusted Pt. 2 to Pt. 2 of the original with a pin. Using the pin as a pivot point, swing your pattern until your waist depth mark coincides with the waistline of the original.

Pin the patterns together in this position. For styles with a casing, trace the casing foldline from the original pattern in red. For styles with darts, trace only from Pt. 2 to the dart. Then slide your pattern over, matching your adjusted Pt. 1 to Pt. 1 of the original, while you trace the remainder of the waistline.

This is your center front waist depth. If the center front is lower than the high side, make an arrow pointing DOWN in front of the difference. If the center front is higher than the high side, make an arrow pointing UP in front of the difference.

Extend the center front seamline upward for about 2" above Pt. 1 in blue. Using a triangle, draw a blue guide line at right angles to the center front seamline from Pt. 2 to the center front. Label Pt. A where the blue lines meet. Extend the blue line to meet your adjusted side seamline as necessary.

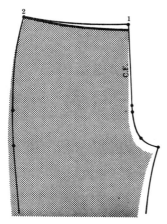

NOTE: If your waistline is *above* Pt. A, curve the center front seamline so that it meets the waistline at a right angle. Redraw, starting 1" below Pt. A, as shown. This follows the shape of your rounded tummy and eliminates the point that would otherwise occur when the center front seams are joined.

Back

Enter floor-to-waist measure
of your higher side (A-3 or A-4) . . . . —————

Enter floor-to-waist measure
of center back (A-2) . . . . —————

Find the difference . . . . [   ]

This is your center back waist depth.

If the center back is lower than the high side, make an arrow pointing DOWN in front of the difference.

If the center back is higher than the high side, a correction is required. In this case use zero as your back waist depth.

Mark your center back waist depth and redraw your back waistline in the same manner as on the front pattern. A waist depth of zero coincides with Pt. A.

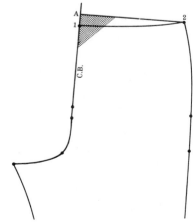

6. Wedge

The amount of wedge affects the hang of the pant legs. Excessive back wedge is a major cause of sags under the seat.

Back

Using a triangle, draw a blue line at right angles to the center back seamline from your adjusted Pt. 3 to the center back. This is the *wedge line*. Label We.L.

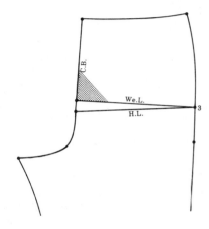

Enter your center back waist
indentation (A-6) . . . . —————

Enter your back wedge from
the chart below . . . . [   ]

C.B. Waist Indentation (A-6)	Back Wedge	
	Hip to 40"	Hip over 40"
Up to 1-1/4"	1/2"	5/8"
1-1/2" to 2"	3/4"	7/8"
Over 2"	1"	1-1/8"

Measure UP from Pt. 11 at the **center back** and mark your back wedge in blue.

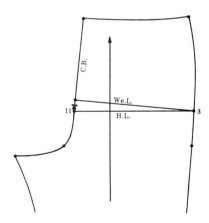

Cut the pattern along the wedge line **from the center back to your adjusted Pt. 3.** **If your mark is** *below* the wedge line, **overlap the upper pattern** section until the wedge line meets your blue mark. Tape in place.

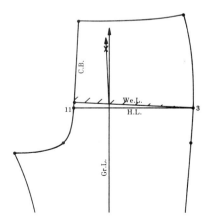

If your mark is *above* the wedge line, measure the distance from your mark to the wedge line and record . . . Spread the pattern sections apart at the **center back** the amount recorded. Place a strip of **pattern paper** underneath and tape in place.

Clip the right edge of the paper to **your adjusted** Pt. 3 so the pattern will lie flat. Cross out the **grainline** above the wedge line and **redraw so it is** straight and continuous with the original **grainline.**

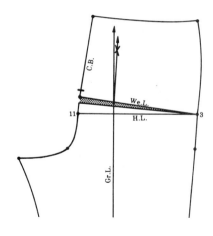

Front

Enter your center front waist indentation (A-5) . . . . _____

Enter your front wedge from the chart below . . . . [ ]

C.F. Waist Indentation (A-5)	Front Wedge	
	Hip to 40"	Hip over 40"
Less than 3/4"	1/4"	3/8"
3/4" to 1-1/4"	1/2"	5/8"
Over 1-1/4"	3/4"	7/8"

Mark the front pattern and adjust the front wedge in the same manner as the back.

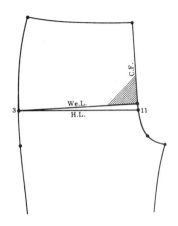

7. Crotch Point Extension

This is seldom a problem on the front pattern but it is wise to check the back pattern. Sufficient crotch point extension is necessary to assure adequate sitting room without binding.

Measure your back pattern width
at the hipline, from your adjusted
Pt. 3 to Pt. 11 and record . . . . _____

Divide by 2 . . . . _____

Enter your deduction from the
chart below . . . . _____

Find the difference . . . . [   ]

This is your back crotch point extension.

C.B. Waist Indentation (A-6)	Deduction	
	Hip to 40"	Hip over 40"
Less than 1-1/2"	1/2"	zero
1-1/2" to 2"	1/4"	zero
Over 2"	zero	zero

Draw the *center line* on the back pattern in blue, parallel to the grainline, from Pt. 11 to the kneeline. Label C.L.

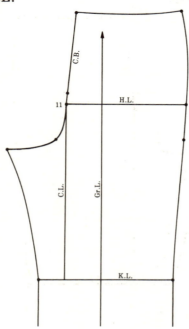

Measure from the center line toward the crotch point and mark your *back crotch point extension* in blue. Extend this mark downward, parallel to the grainline for about 2".

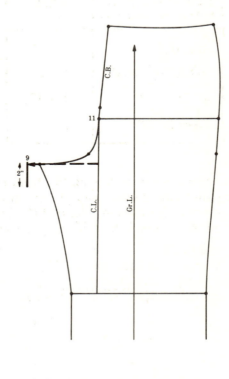

8. Inseam

The position and length of the back inseam greatly affect the hang of the pants.

Enter your back crotch point
extension from the box in step 7 . . . . _____

Divide by 2 . . . . _____

Extra ease (See note below) . . . . _____

Total . . . . [   ]

This is your back knee extension.

NOTE: *Extra ease is needed for people with certain figure characteristics.* Consider your stance when standing at ease.

If your legs *do not touch*, or if they barely touch at the top *only*, you probably do not need any extra ease. Enter zero.

If your legs *touch at the knees* or if they *touch at the middle of the thighs*, determine your extra ease from the chart below.

Back crotch point extension (Step 7)	Extra Ease
Up to 4"	1-1/4"
4-1/4" to 4-3/4"	1-1/2"
5" to 5-1/2"	1-3/4"
Over 5-1/2"	2"

Measure from the center line on the back pattern, along the knee line toward the left, and mark your *back knee extension* in blue. Extend the knee line to your mark, as needed. This is your adjusted Pt. 8.

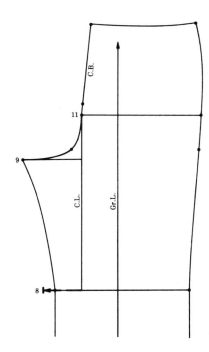

It is important for the length of the back inseam to have the correct relationship to the length of the front inseam. By making the back shorter than the front and stretching the back to fit in the sewing, the back crotch seam curves lower under the seat and reduces clinging below the hipline.

Measure the inseam of the *front* pattern from Pt. 8 to Pt. 9 and record .... _____

Deduction . . . . 1/2"

Find the difference . . . . [ ]

This is the length your back upper inseam should be.

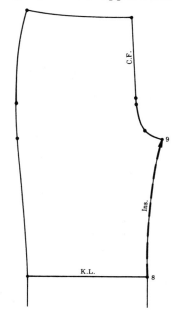

Measure upward from your adjusted Pt. 8 on the back pattern, toward the crotch point and mark the length your *back upper inseam* should be, in blue, across the blue line that marks your crotch point extension. Your adjusted Pt. 9 is where these blue lines intersect.

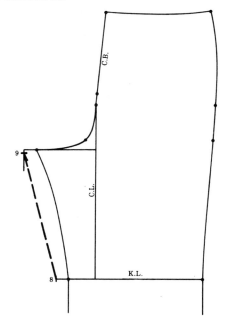

Place your back pattern on top of the original pattern, matching your adjusted Pt. 9 to Pt. 9 of the original with a pin. Using the pin as a pivot point, swing your pattern until your adjusted Pt. 8 coincides with the inseam of the original. Pin the patterns together in this position and trace the *upper inseam* from the original onto your pattern in red, from Pt. 8 to Pt. 9. Write STRETCH between Pt. 8 and Pt. 9.

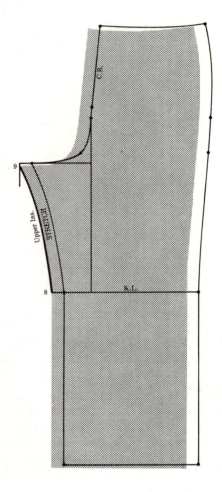

Draw the *lower inseam* in red, parallel to the original, from your adjusted Pt. 8 to the hemline.

9. Crotch Curve

If the position of the back crotch point was changed, it is necessary to re-draw the curve from the crotch point to the hipline.

First draw a blue line at right angles to the grainline from your adjusted Pt. 9 to the center line. This is your *adjusted crotchline*. Label Pt. X where the crotchline meets the center line.

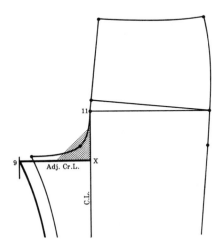

Draw a diagonal guide line in blue, at a 45 degree angle to the crotchline, from Pt. X to the curve, as shown.

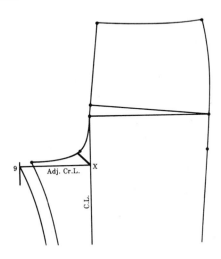

Enter your back crotch
point extension from the box in step 7 . . . . _____

Divide by 4 . . . . [ ]

This is the length your back diagonal should be.

Measure from Pt. X toward the crotch curve and mark the length your *back diagonal* should be, in blue. The point where this mark crosses the diagonal guide line is your adjusted Pt. 10.

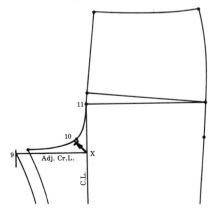

Locate Pt. 10 on the original pattern back as shown here.

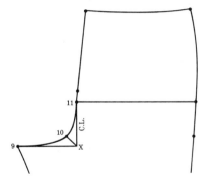

Place your back pattern on top of the original, matching your adjusted Pt. 10 to Pt. 10 of the original with a pin. Using the pin as a pivot point, swing your pattern until your adjusted Pt. 9 coincides with Pt. 9 of the original, as closely as possible. Trace your *crotch curve* from the original, in red, from Pt. 10 to Pt. 9.

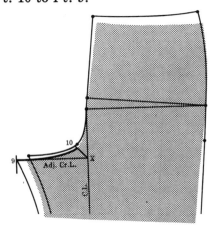

Swing your pattern again from Pt. 10, until your pattern coincides with the original center seamline at Pt. 11. Trace the crotch curve from Pt. 10 to Pt. 11. Continue in a smooth line to meet the center back seamline at Pt. 12.

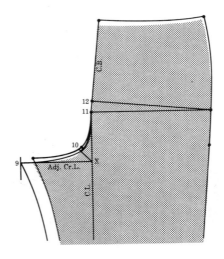

10. Side Seam

Consider the shape of your silhouette. If you have a high hip bulge or a side thigh bulge, you probably need to re-shape your side seamlines.

High Hip Bulge

If your high hip circumference (A-8) is greater than your full hip circumference (A-9), check the pattern width at the high hipline.

On the front and back patterns, measure from Pt. 2 downward along the side seamline 3" and mark the high hip point in blue. Draw the high hipline from this mark to the center front and center back seamlines, at right angles to the center seamlines.

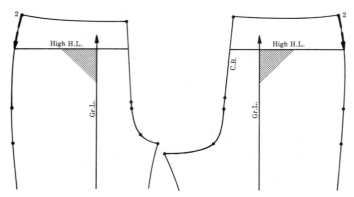

Enter your high hip circumference (A-8) . . _____

Enter 1" ease for woven fabric; zero for knits . . . . _____

Find total . . . . _____

Divide by 2 . . . . [   ]

This is your *minimum* pattern width at high hipline.

Place your front and back patterns side by side, matching adjusted side seamlines at the high hip point. Pin the patterns together at this point. Measure from the center back seamline along the high hipline, toward the center front and mark your *minimum pattern width* at high hipline in blue.

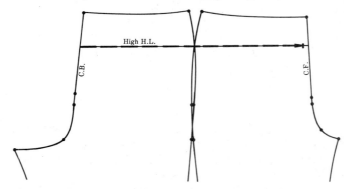

If your mark is to the left of the center front seamline, no further adjustment is required. If your mark is to the right of the center front seamline, measure the distance from your mark to the center front and record . . . . . . _____

Divide by 4 . . . . [   ]

This is the amount of adjustment for each pattern piece.

Re-mark your side seamlines OUT this amount from the initial adjusted side seamline at the high hipline on front and back patterns in blue.

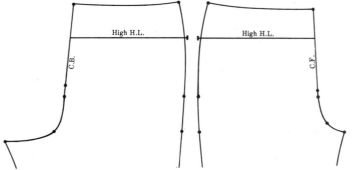

Place your front pattern on top of the original pattern matching side seamlines at the high hip point with a pin. Using the pin as a pivot point, swing your pattern until your adjusted Pt. 3 coincides with the side seamline of the original pattern.

Re-trace your side seamline from Pt. 3 to the high hip point. Use a contrasting color, such as violet.

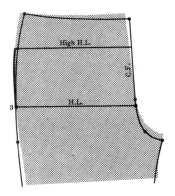

Now swing the pattern from the high hip point until your adjusted Pt. 2 coincides with the side seamlines of the original pattern. Re-trace your side seamline from Pt. 2 to the high hip point. Your side seamline should be a smooth curve. Round off any angles that may have occurred.

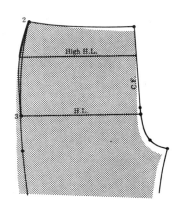

Re-trace the side seamline onto your back pattern from Pt. 2 to Pt. 3 in the same way. Cross out the red lines that no longer apply.

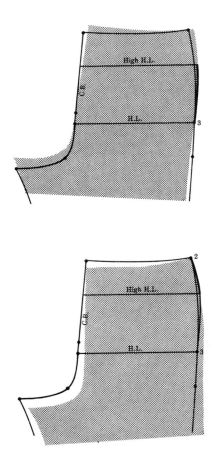

If you have a high hip bulge *combined with* a side thigh bulge, proceed to the next section. If you have a high hip bulge *without* side thigh bulge, re-draw your side seamlines below the hipline as follows:

Place your front pattern on top of the original pattern, matching your *adjusted Pt. 3* to *Pt. 4* of the original with a pin. Using the pin as a pivot point, swing your pattern until your adjusted Pt. 5 coincides with the side seamline of the original pattern. In this position, re-trace your side seamline from Pt. 3 to Pt. 5 in the contrast color.

Re-trace the side seamline onto your back pattern from Pt. 3 to Pt. 5 in the same way. Cross out the red lines that no longer apply.

Side Thigh Bulge

Too close a fit at the side seams accentuates side thigh bulges. Moderate and narrow leg styles may taper more sharply from hip to knee than is becoming for you. Consider re-shaping your side seamline. If wide leg styles are popular, you may wish to re-draw your side seamlines parallel to the grainline from Pt. 3 to the hemline.

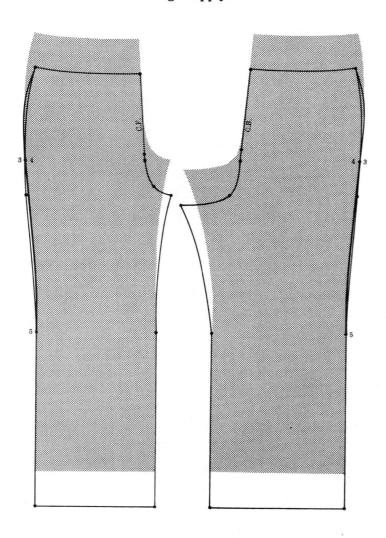

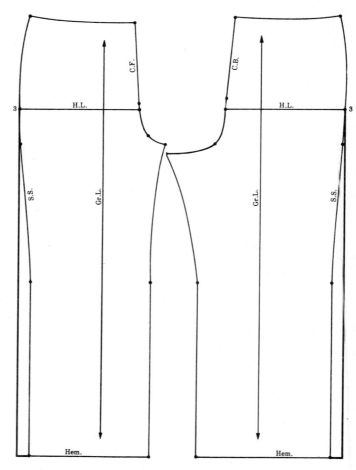

For a moderate pantleg width, draw a blue guide line parallel to the grainline from Pt. 3 to the hemline. Mark your side seamline IN 1" to 2" from the guideline at the knee. Label Pt. 5. Draw your side seamlines parallel to the guideline from your adjusted Pt. 5 to the hem. Re-trace the side seamlines from your adjusted Pt. 4 to the adjusted Pt. 5 by pivoting, as described previously.

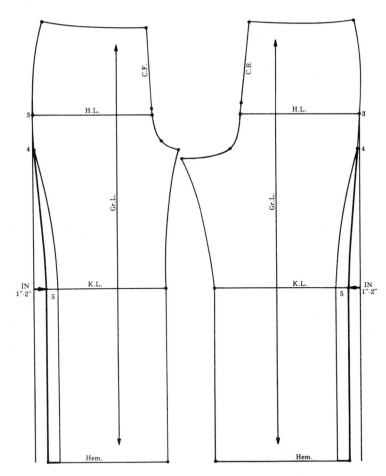

Bow-Legs

The pantleg adjustments recommended for people with side thigh bulge also apply to people with bow-legs. If you have this figure characteristic, provide ample width at the knee by reshaping your side seamlines as shown above.

Changes for Uneven Figures

After adjusting the pattern to the measurements of your higher or larger side, consider the degree of difference between your right and left sides. If the difference is slight, it may not cause a noticeable difference in the hang of the pants.

It is usually advisable to try the pattern with the same adjustment on both sides for the first try-on. If the difference *is* enough to be obvious, mark a second set of stitching lines for the low side in a contrasting color, on the same pattern.

One High Hip

Having one hip higher than the other is the most common uneven figure characteristic. The higher

side is usually a little wider also. This shows up in the body measurements from floor to waist. If you have a difference of one-half inch or more between left and right sides (A-3 and A-4), you will probably need to mark a separate adjustment for the low side.

Keep the width at the waist the same for both sides by making a short blue guide line through your adjusted Pt. 2, parallel to the center seamline. Measure down from Pt. 2 of the high side and mark the amount of difference. Label Pt. 2 for the low side where the marks cross.

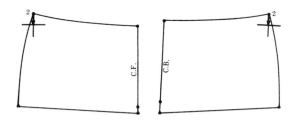

Re-draw your waistline from the low Pt. 2 to Pt. 1. Re-draw the side seamline from the low Pt. 2 to Pt. 3. Use a contrasting color, such as green. Be sure to label which is right and which is left.

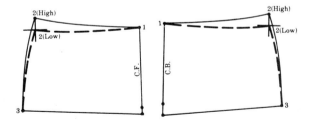

One Wide Hip Or One Wide Thigh

It is rarely advisable to make a difference in width for right and left sides until you have tested your pattern in a try-on. If you suspect you will need to do this, allow double seam allowance for the larger side.

Now it's break time again.

Making Test Pants

COMPLETING THE PATTERN FOR TEST PANTS

Trace the final stitching lines of your adjusted pattern onto fresh pattern paper, omitting the guide lines. Retain the adjusted pattern for reference.

Place carbon paper face down on a piece of pattern paper and place the adjusted pattern on top, face up. Pin the layers together to prevent slipping.

Trace all stitching lines, grainlines, hemlines and hiplines. Trace cross-marks at Points 4, 5, 8, 9, and 10. Unpin the patterns.

Crease Line

Locate the center of the pantleg on the front and back pattern by folding in half at the hemline.

Lightly crease from hem to crotchline. This is the *crease line*. It should be parallel to the grainline.

Cutting Lines

Draw cutting lines on each pattern piece, parallel to the stitching lines. Allow 1" for seams and 2" for hems. This provides room for possible corrections.

If your pattern has a casing, label the waistline FOLDLINE FOR CASING. Add 2½" above the fold line to make the casing. Fold the pattern under on the fold line and trace the side and center seamlines for 2½". Indicate space for the insertion of elastic at the center back, by making two dots on the center back seamline. Make one at the fold line and the other 1¼" away, on the casing. Label LEAVE OPEN BETWEEN DOTS.

COMPLETED PATTERN FOR STYLES WITH CASING

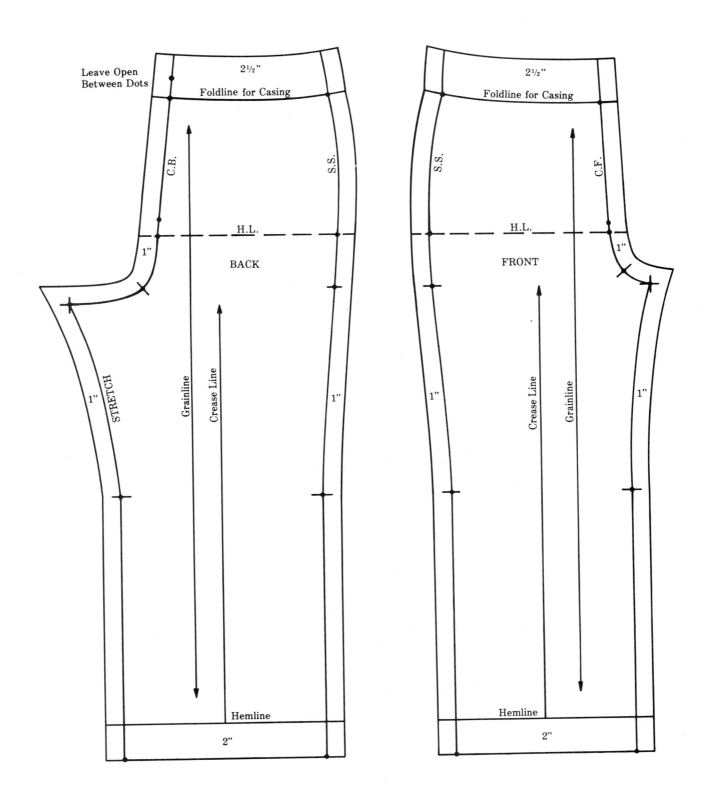

COMPLETED PATTERN FOR STYLES WITH DARTS

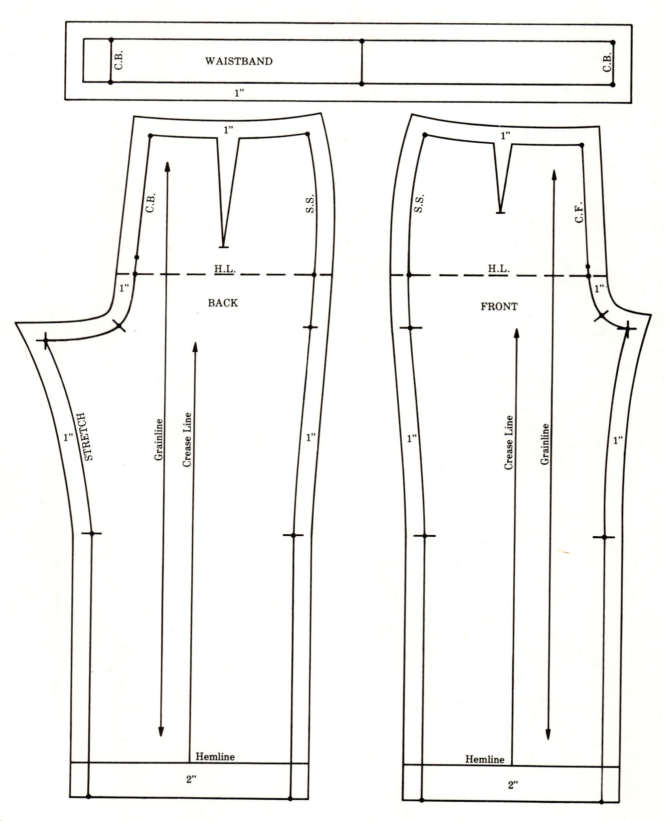

LAYOUT, CUTTING, AND MARKING

If the crosswise ends of the fabric are uneven, straighten by tearing or cutting along a pulled thread. Fold fabric in half lengthwise, right sides together. Pin the edges together to prevent slipping.

Place a layer of graphite paper or dressmaker's carbon face up, *under* the fabric and another layer face down, *on top* of the fabric.

Lay the pattern on top, face up. Pin in place, making sure that the grainlines are parallel to the fold of the fabric.

Trace all stitching lines, hemlines, foldlines, and grainlines onto the fabric with a smooth tracing wheel. Lay a ruler along the straight lines to help you trace them straight. Trace a cross at each end of the crease line. Trace the cross marks at points 3, 4, 5, 8, 9, 10, and 11.

Remove the carbon paper carefully, without changing the position of the pattern on the fabric. Cut out the fabric along the cutting lines.

Using cotton thread of a contrasting color, machine baste along the waistline so it is visible on the outside. Baste through the crossmarks at points 3, 4, 5, 8, 9, 10, and 11. Mark each end of the crease line with a tailor tack.

CONSTRUCTION

Join fronts to backs along inseams, right sides together. Match corresponding crossmarks, stretching back to fit. Baste from hem to crotch, by machine, with cotton thread of contrasting color. *Accuracy in matching and stitching is important!* Press seams open.

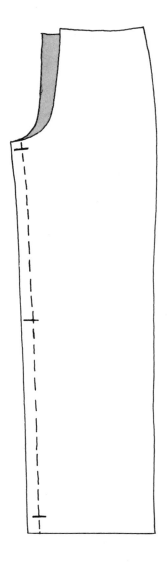

Join crotch seams, right sides together, with corresponding points matching. Leave space open for zipper. If there is a casing, leave center back seam open between dots. TRIM SEAM TO 3/8" ALONG THE CROTCH CURVE BELOW THE HIPLINE MARKS. A seam wider than this on the curve of the crotch will interfere with the fit. Press seams open *above* the hipline but *not* below.

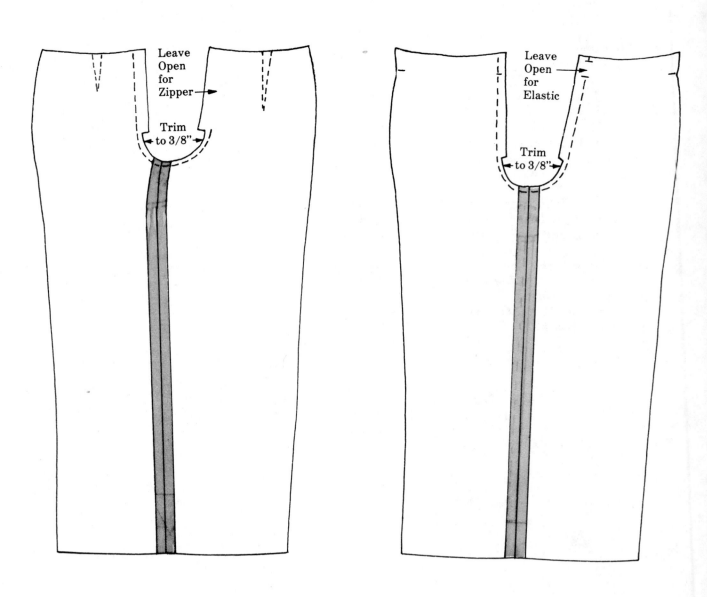

Match side seams of each pant leg, right sides together, starting at the hemline. Baste and press seams open lightly.

For pants with elastic, turn the casing inside along the fold line. The finished width of the casing should be ¼" more than the width of the elastic. If ¾" elastic is used, baste 1" from the fold. If 1" elastic is used, baste 1¼" from the fold. It is not necessary to turn under the raw edge of the fabric while testing.

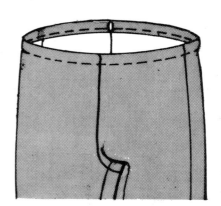

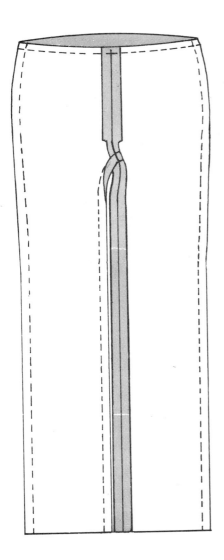

Use firm non-roll type elastic. Be sure to preshrink the elastic before cutting because many elastics shrink greatly. Cut the elastic equal to your waist measure (A-7). You can overlap it until it is as snug as desired.

Fasten a safety pin onto the end of the elastic and insert through the opening in the center back seam. Pull the elastic through the casing. Overlap the ends and pin together. Try on the pants and adjust the elastic until it is as snug as is comfortable.

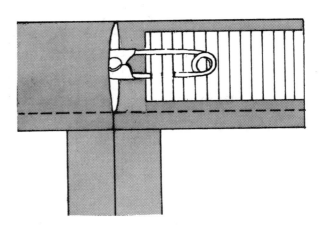

For pants with darts, fold darts through center, bringing stitching lines together. Machine baste along stitching lines from waistline to point of each dart. Often the waistline darts are slightly curved. Take care to stitch them accurately. Press toward center front or center back.

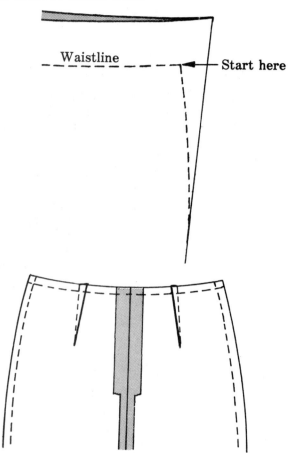

Fold waistband in half lengthwise and pin both edges to the waistline, right sides together, matching corresponding marks. Ease waistline onto band by pulling up the excess fullness on the basting thread that was stitched into the waistline. Hand baste in place accurately. Press all seam allowances upward. Leave the inside unfinished while testing.

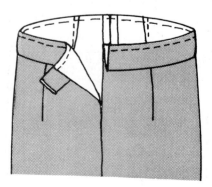

Turn up the hem on the hemline and baste in place, without turning under the raw edge.

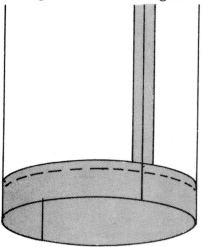

With the pants right side out, fold on the crease-lines between tailor tacks. Press the creases lightly on the folds. Hang by the hems, on a pants hanger.

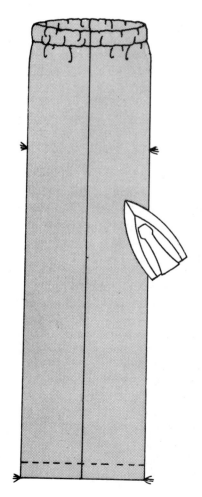

Evaluating the Fit

If you carried out all the instructions carefully, your test pants should be close to perfect fit. But it is only human to be imperfect, and it is likely there is something you will need to change.

It is difficult to get precise body measurements. The body fluctuates easily, especially after a meal. Any error in taking measurements or in applying the measurements to the pattern will show up when you try on your test pants. Some imperfections in fit can be traced to sewing errors.

The try-on may show the need for special adjustments you didn't think would apply to you. Many people don't realize they have figure faults until they try to adjust a pattern to perfect fit. This is especially true for uneven figures. When you know what to look for, you can analyze the fitting problems and correct them.

CRITERIA OF PERFECT FIT

The two criteria of perfect fit are *comfort* and *appearance*. Your pants should feel comfortable whether you are standing, sitting, or in motion. There should be no feeling of tightness or binding.

A becoming fit emphasizes your best features and minimizes figure faults. The pants should hang smoothly, without excess fullness, sagging, or tension wrinkles. The vertical seams should appear centered on the body. The seams and creases should hang straight and perpendicular to the floor. The lengthwise grain of the fabric should have a vertical alignment, with the crosswise grain horizontal in the major areas of each garment section.

Since pants hang from the waist, *do not* try to evaluate the fit without putting elastic in the casing or putting on the waistband. It would be a mistake to do otherwise, as you cannot tell if the waistline curve and ease are right for you without the elastic or waistband to hold the waistline in place on your body. In pants with elastic in a casing, the *top* of the casing should rest at the natural waistline. In pants with a waistband, the waistline *seam* should rest at the natural waistline.

THE TRY-ON

When you try on your test pants, be sure to wear the same undergarments you did when you were measured. Put the pants on *right side out*. Pin together the zipper opening, matching seamline markings. Pin the waistband together, matching markings at the lap.

Checking for Comfort

Test for comfort by sitting and walking, as well as standing still in your pants. Any imperfection that makes the pants feel uncomfortable will usually also affect the way they look, but not always. Sometimes they look fine but feel tight at the crotch.

If your pants feel too snug at the crotch, check first that you trimmed the seam allowance on the crotch curve to 3/8" below the hipline. Excess seam allowance on the crotch curve makes pants feel snug. If the crotch feels too snug even after the seams have been properly trimmed, you may need to make a change in the crotch curve. See examples 11 and 22 in Chart C.

If your pants feel too tight at the waist, re-pin the waistband until it feels comfortable. See example 1. If they feel tight around the hips, rip the side seams from waist to crotchline and re-pin, letting out the side seams. See example 18 in Chart C.

Checking Appearance

Look at the fit of your pants in a three-way mirror, if possible, or enlist the help of a friend. Stand erect and note any wrinkles, sagging, or bulging of the fabric. Tension wrinkles indicate pulling where the width or length is inadequate. Sags, folds, and bulges indicate excessive width or length.

Observe the alignment of seams, creases, and fabric grain. The crosswise grain should be in a horizontal position at the hipline. The creases should be on the lengthwise grain of the fabric. If the pants were properly cut and constructed, any crease or seamline that does not hang straight and perpendicular to the floor indicates improper proportions in some part of the pattern, or a curve that does not follow the curve of your figure as it should.

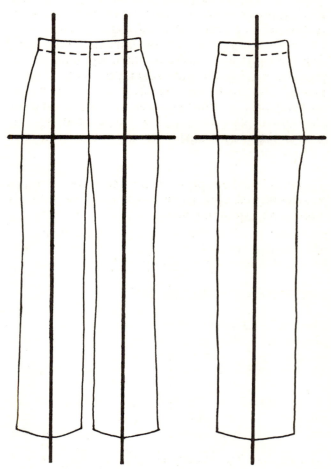

If an imperfection is apparent on one side only, it is either because the two sides of your body are not identical or because the pants are not constructed exactly the same on both sides.

Judging the Fit

The main lengths and widths must be adequate before you can accurately judge the hang of the pants. Compare the fit of your pants to the illustrations. Evaluate the waist and hip circumference and the crotch depth from the standpoint of comfort and appearance. Carry out the changes to correct any faults in these areas before proceeding.

It is impossible to evaluate the finer points as long as the pants are too snug at the waist or hip, or if the crotch depth is too short. After you have made needed corrections in waist and hip circumference and in crotch depth, try the pants on again and analyze any remaining imperfections.

Analyzing Fitting Faults

Fitting faults may be due to any one of several factors, or to a combination of factors. The effects of certain corrections can be approximated by pulling the pants up or down on the body, pinning in a tuck, or ripping the side seam part way. Where possible, do this to test the effect of the change you contemplate. At the same time, you can estimate the amount of change. If the suggested test improves the fit, make the corresponding correction on your pattern.

To test the effect of lowering the waist depth, a wedge-shaped tuck is pinned across the front or back, just below the waist.

To test the effect of decreasing the wedge, a wedge-shaped tuck is pinned along the hipline on front or back.

To test the effect of decreasing crotch depth, an even tuck is pinned *all around* the hipline.

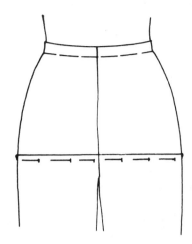

When you have identified the fitting fault and its probable cause and correction, you must decide on the amount of correction. If pinning ½" of fabric into a tuck or raising the pants ½" on the body made the fault disappear, you probably need ½" correction. Where the pants are very tight over the hip, you may rip the side seams to release the tension. If the seams each spread ½", you probably need to add at least ¼" on *each* side seam.

Where you cannot estimate the amount of change in this way, try making ¼" change at a time, if you are uncertain how much you need. In some cases 1/8" may be enough to correct the crotch curve or the darts; ½" or more may be needed to correct the main widths and lengths of the pattern.

The examples in CHART C are arranged to show what to look for from the top down. The most likely cause of each fault is listed first. Where more than one solution is given, try one at a time, in the order given. If the change does not improve the fit, take it out. If the change improves but does not eliminate the fault, try additional changes. If your pants look like examples 1, 2, 11, 18, or 22, correct these faults on your pants before you try to evaluate any other feature of the fit. Instructions for carrying out the corrections start on page 60.

CHART C: FITTING FAULTS: CAUSES AND CORRECTIONS

1. Waistband does not reach around waist, or waistband has tension wrinkles; may cause body to bulge out suddenly above the waist. Pants feel tight at waist.

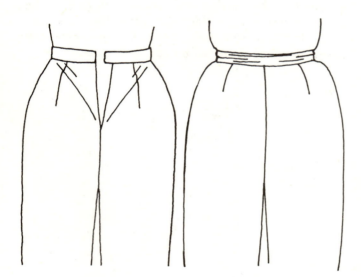

Waist circumference is inadequate. *Test by re-pinning waistband or elastic with less overlap to determine amount.*

Increase length of waistband or elastic. Redistribute ease onto waistband. Dart width may need to be decreased, or you may need to move Pt. 2 OUT on front and back. A narrow waistband is preferred for people who naturally bulge just above the waist.

2. Pants sag below natural waistline or waistband stands away from the body. Pants feel loose at waist. Crotch may hang too low.

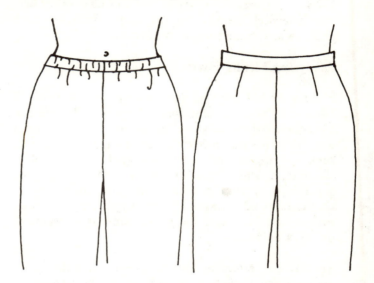

Waist circumference is excessive. *Test by re-pinning waistband or elastic with more overlap to determine amount.*

Decrease length of waistband or elastic. Redistribute ease at waistline seam. Dart width may need to be increased, or you may need to move Pt. 2 IN on front and back.

3. Gathers at waistline are excessive in pants with elastic.

Waist circumference on pants is excessive.

Move Pt. 2 IN on front and back.

NOTE: Persons with a very small waist may add a small dart, extending it through the casing.

4. There are gathers at waistline seam on pants with waistband, even though waistband is not too tight.

Waist circumference of pants is excessive.

Move Pt. 2 IN on front and back. Increase width of darts.

5. Diagonal wrinkles pull from side waist point toward tip of dart.

Dart is too narrow. Width at side waist point inadequate.

Increase width of dart. Move Pt. 2 OUT on front and back.

NOTE: If you have prominent hip bones, use two darts in front, making *side* dart wider than center dart.

6. Diagonal wrinkles pull from top of dart toward side of hip. There may be a bulge of fabric at dart points.

Dart is too wide. Width at side waist point excessive. Darts end too abruptly.

Decrease width of darts and move Pt. 2 IN on front and back. If there is still a bulge at dart points, increase length of darts, or curve darts more, or both. Make sure the sewing ends *at* dart point.

7. Diagonal wrinkles between two darts pull toward top of center dart.

Center dart is too wide and side dart is not wide enough.

Decrease width of center dart and increase width of side dart.

NOTE: If the wrinkles point the opposite direction, reverse the procedure.

8. Diagonal wrinkles pull toward side waist point or hip on one side only.

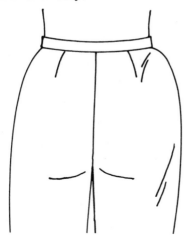

Figure is uneven. One hip is higher than the other. *Test by pulling pants down from waist on high side.*

Move Pt. 2 UP on high side. Perhaps also increase curve of darts and side seamline on high side. See example 21.

9. Side seams pull toward front at waist.

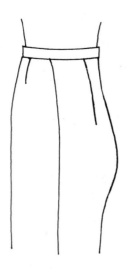

Front darts are too wide and back darts too narrow.

Decrease width of front darts and increase width of back darts.

10. Side seams pull toward back at waist.

Back darts too wide and front darts too narrow.

Decrease width of back darts and increase width of front darts.

11. Waistline of pants does not reach natural waistline. Crotch is snug.

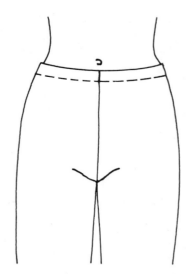

Crotch depth is too short. *Test by pulling pants down on body.*

Increase crotch depth on adjustment lines, same amount on front and back.

12. Pants dip below natural waistline at center front, even though waistband or elastic is comfortably snug.

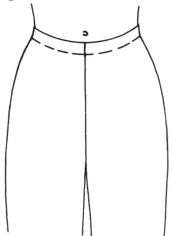

Waist depth is too low at center front or front wedge may be too narrow.

Move Pt. 1 UP at center front or increase front wedge. See example 31.

13. Pants rise above natural waistline at center front. When held at natural waistline, front crotch sags too low or forms horizontal fold across front crotch area.

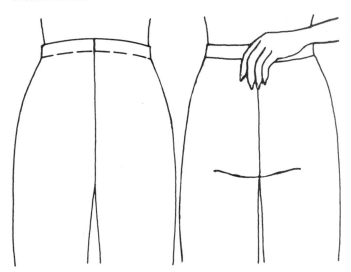

Waist depth is too high at center front or front wedge too wide. *Test wedge by pinning in a tuck along hipline at center front, tapering to nothing at sides.*

Move Pt. 1 DOWN at center front or decrease front wedge. See example 32.

14. Pants dip below natural waistline at center back. Waistline pulls down excessively at center back when sitting.

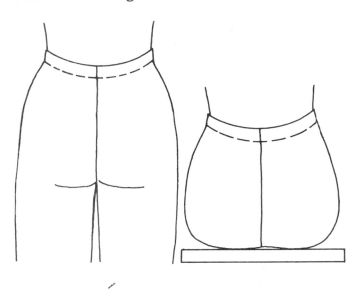

Waistband or elastic may not be snug enough. *Test by re-pinning with more overlap.* **If pants still dip at center back, the waist depth is too low or back wedge too narrow. Possibly the crotch depth is too short or back crotch point extension inadequate.** *Be sure hip circumference is ample.*

Move Pt. 1 UP at center back or increase back wedge. See example 33.

15. Pants sag into folds just below waist at center back, even though high hip circumference is adequate.

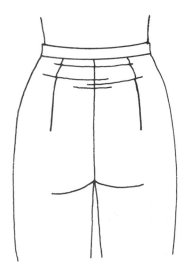

49

Waist depth is too high at center back or back wedge too wide. *Test waist depth by pinning in a tuck just below the waist at center back, tapering to nothing at sides. Test wedge by pinning in a tuck along hipline, tapering to nothing at sides. Observe the effect on the hang of the creases. See examples 16 and 34.*

Move Pt. 1 DOWN at center back or decrease back wedge.

16.   **Tension wrinkles pull across high hip area in front or back. Pants may ride up forming horizontal wrinkles just below waist. Diagonal wrinkles may pull toward high hip.**

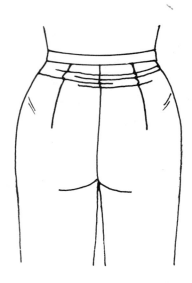

Width is inadequate at high hipline and perhaps also at waistline. *Test by ripping darts. If strain is still apparent, rip side seams from waist to hipline.*

Curve front darts more. Shorten front darts. If there are two darts in back, shorten the *side* darts to 3" or 4" length and curve them. If tension still exists, decrease dart width. Move Pt. 2 OUT on front and back. If figure is larger at high hip than at seat level, redraw side seam curve, increasing width at high hipline. *Be sure width is adequate at full hipline.*

17.   **Pants are loose at high hipline.**

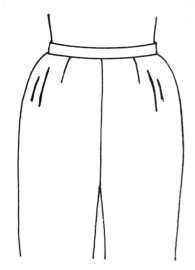

Width at high hipline is excessive and perhaps also at the waistline.

Make less curve on front darts. Lengthen darts. Make less curve on side seam at high hipline. See example 4.

18.   **Tension wrinkles pull across hipline. Pants may feel tight around hips, especially when sitting.**

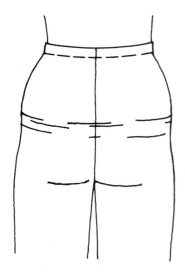

Hip circumference is inadequate. *Test by ripping side seams from waist to crotch, to release the tension. Pin together taking up less seam allowance.*

Move Pt. 3 OUT on front and back. Move Pt. 4 OUT same amount. Perhaps increase back crotch point extension also, at Pt. 9.

19. Fabric bulges at hipline or may hang in vertical folds. There is more than enough width at hipline when sitting.

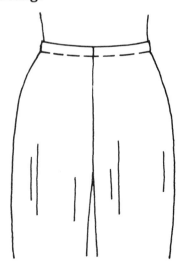

Hip circumference is excessive. *Test by pinning vertical tuck at side seams.*

Move Pt. 3 IN on front and back. Move Pt. 4 IN same amount. Perhaps decrease back crotch point extension also, at Pt. 9.

NOTE: The figure that is larger at high hip than at seat level requires more ease at the hipline than the average. Too close a fit at hipline would be unbecoming.

20. Pants bulge or ripple at side seams over hip.

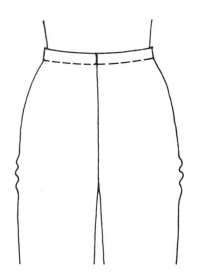

Too much curve on side seamline.

Redraw side seamlines with less curve over hip.

21. Pants snug over one hip or thigh and loose on the other side.

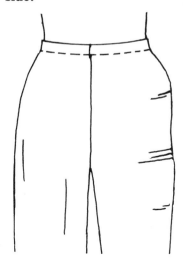

Figure is uneven. One hip or one thigh is wider than the other. *Test by ripping side seam on tight side and pinning side seam tighter on loose side.*

Move Pt. 3 and Pt. 4 OUT on the wide side and move Pt. 3 and Pt. 4 IN on the smaller side. Perhaps increase curve of side seam or darts on the wide side and decrease curves on the smaller side.

22. Diagonal wrinkles pull down toward crotch in front. Pants may cling under seat. Crotch feels snug even though crotch seam has been trimmed to 3/8".

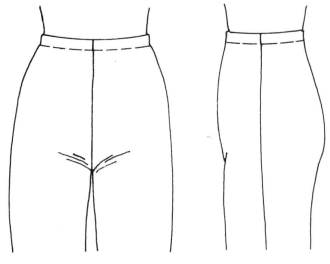

Crotch depth is too short. *Test by pulling pants down on body.*

Increase crotch depth on adjustment line, same amount on front and back.

23. Crotch hangs too low on body. An excessive horizontal fold may form across front crotch when bending forward.

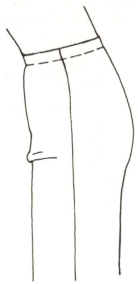

Crotch depth is too long. *Test by pinning an even tuck all around hipline.*

Decrease crotch depth on adjustment lines, same amount on front and back. See example 13.

24. Horizontal tension wrinkles pull toward front crotch. Pants cling to inside of thigh. Side seams may curve forward over thighs.

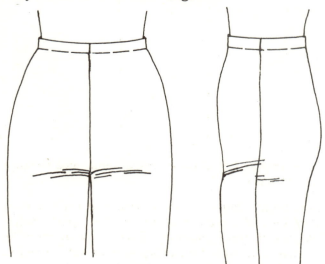

Inadequate width at crotch point.

Increase *back* crotch point extension at Pt. 9. If thighs are full at front or inner side, also increase front crotch point extension at Pt. 9. See example 18.

25. Pants too full over front crotch area and inside of leg in front.

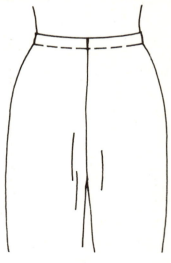

Front crotch curve is too shallow or front crotch point extension is excessive.

Increase depth of curve on front crotch seam by making shorter diagonal at Pt. 10. Decrease crotch point extension at Pt. 9 in back, in front, or both.

26. Diagonal wrinkles sag downward from front crotch point, although pantlegs *do not* cling to inside of leg.

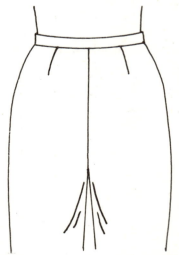

Waistline not curved enough. Back crotch point too high, back crotch point extension inadequate. *Test waistline curve by lifting pants at waist, about 4" from center front.*

Increase curve of waistline by dipping it slightly, 4" from center front. Move Pt. 9 DOWN in *back*. Increase *back* crotch point extension at Pt. 9. See example 27.

27. Pants cling or cup under seat, although circumference at hip is adequate. There may be diagonal wrinkles pulling toward crotch in back.

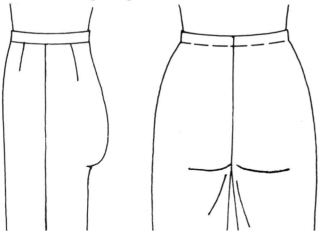

Inadequate width at crotch point.

Increase back crotch point extension at Pt. 9. See example 28.

28. Diagonal wrinkles pull toward crotch and inside of upper leg in back.

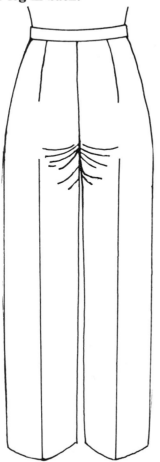

Back crotch point extension may be inadequate or back crotch curve may be too high or too shallow.

Increase back crotch point extension at Pt. 9. Lower back crotch curve by moving Pt. 9 DOWN and redraw crotch curve to increase depth of curve by making shorter diagonal at Pt. 10.

Be sure crotch depth and width at inseams are adequate. See examples 22 and 30.

29. Pants are too full at back leg, just below seat.

Excessive width at back crotch point, and perhaps also at knee.

Test crotch point width by pinning a vertical tuck over seat at crotch level, or carefully pin a vertical tuck at top of inseam. Test width at knee by pinning a vertical tuck along side seams, taking in pants at knee, tapering to nothing at hipline.

Decrease back crotch point extension at Pt. 9 and probably also at Pt. 8 and Pt. 7 on back only. Decrease pantleg width at Pt. 5 and 6 on front and back.

30. Pants cling to inside of leg. Creases pull inward toward hems. There may be tension wrinkles pulling toward inside of leg. Inseams may ripple below crotch.

31. Front creases swing inward at hems. There may be a diagonal fold sagging from the tummy downward and backward toward the side.

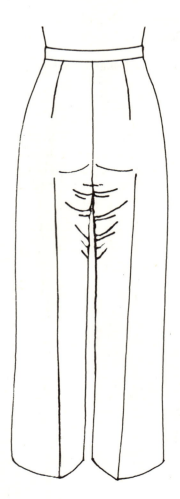

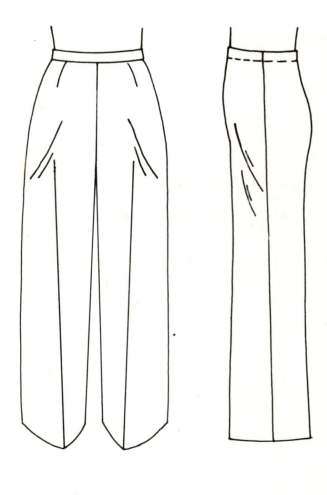

Inseam too tapered, inadequate width at inseam at knee, especially if figure is knock-kneed or if thighs are full. *Test by ripping inseams. Pin inseams together taking up less seam allowance.*

Extend width of pantleg on back only at Pt. 8. Add same amount at Pt. 7. If pantlegs become too wide, subtract from side seam width at Pt. 5 and Pt. 6 on back and front. If pants still cling at inseam, extend width of pantleg on front inseam at Pt. 7 and Pt. 8.

Front wedge may be too narrow or front waist depth too low, especially for a prominent abdomen.

Increase front wedge or move Pt. 1 UP at center front. See example 12.

32. **Front creases swing outward at hems. An excessive fold of fabric may form across front crotch when bending forward.**

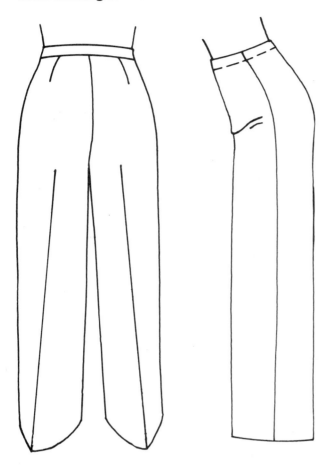

Front wedges are too wide or front waist depth too high. *Check wedge by pinning a wedge-shaped tuck along front hipline, tapering to nothing at sides. Check waist depth by pinning a tuck just below the waist at center front, tapering to nothing at sides.*

Decrease front wedge or move Pt. 1 DOWN at center front. See example 13.

33. **Creases swing inward at hems even though pants *do not* cling against insides of legs. Pants pull down excessively in back when sitting. Side seams may swing backward at hems.**

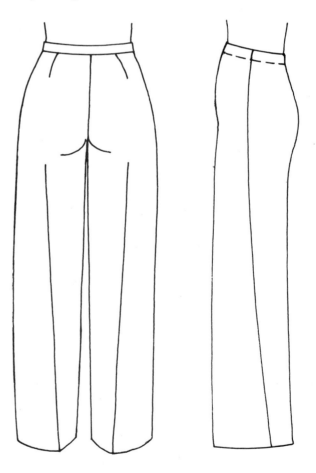

Back wedge too narrow.

Increase back wedge. See example 14.

34. Pants sag in back. May form folds under seat. May sag diagonally toward knees. Back creases may swing out at hems. Side seams may swing forward at hems.

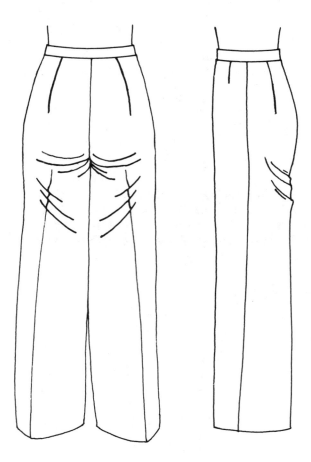

Back wedge too wide. *Test by pinning a wedge-shaped tuck along hipline at center back, tapering to nothing at sides.*

Decrease back wedge. Usually also move Pt. 9 DOWN and redraw back crotch curve with shorter diagonal at Pt. 10.

35. Pantlegs cling against thighs at sides or rest against sides of knees.

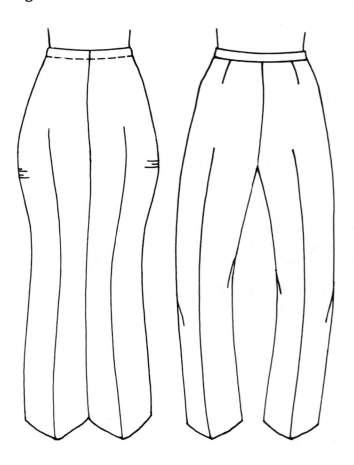

Side seams too tapered for figure with prominent side thigh bulge or for bow-legs.

Move Pt. 5 and Pt. 6 OUT, same amount on front and back. *Make sure hip circumference is ample.*

36. Pantlegs rest on back of leg at calf. Diagonal wrinkles sag toward calf. Side seam follows curve of leg.

Posture is faulty. Knees are extended backward, calves protrude in back, thighs protrude in front. Pantleg width too narrow. *Be sure hip circumference and crotch point extensions are adequate.*

Move Pt. 5 and Pt. 6 OUT same amount on front and back. Avoid narrow pantleg styles.

37. Pantlegs break above foot. Hems rest on instep.

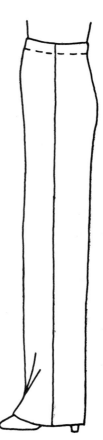

Pantlegs too long.

Move Pt. 6 and Pt. 7 UP, same amount on front and back. Redraw hemline.

38. Side seam curves forward at hem and looks puckered on back.

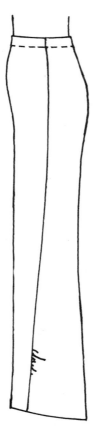

Front pantleg is shorter than back. Front was stretched or back eased into seam during stitching.

Move Pt. 6 and Pt. 7 DOWN on front and redraw front hemline, making front and back same length from knee to hem.

39. Side seam curves backward at hem and looks puckered on front.

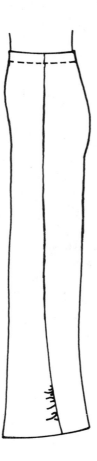

Back pantleg is shorter than front. Back was stretched or front was eased into seam during stitching.

Move Pt. 6 and Pt. 7 DOWN on back and redraw back hemline, making front and back same length from knee to hem.

40. Pantlegs look twisted. Side seam curves forward and inseam curves backward toward hem, or side seam curves backward and inseam curves forward toward hem. This may happen on one pantleg only.

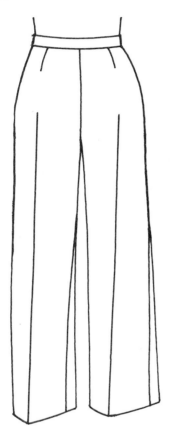

Pantlegs were cut or stitched off-grain. *Check grain position by ravelling a thread from edge of seam.*

Rip off-grain seams, re-match along the straight grain, and re-baste.

Making Corrections

When you have identified your fitting faults and have tested the proposed corrections where possible, by pinning in the proposed change on your test pants, then write down all the changes you decide to carry out, before removing the pins.

POINT-BY-POINT NOTATION

The Point-by-Point system makes it easy to describe the adjustments accurately and concisely, like shorthand. List the location, the direction, and the amount of the adjustments right on your pattern. Record which try-on they apply to and the date. For example, the corrections for your first two try-ons might read like this:

I. 5/24/78 - red lines

Pt. 2 OUT ¼" F & B

+½" F & B Adj. Lines (Spread)

II. 5/26/78 — blue lines

Pt. 1 DOWN ½" at CB

−¾" B Wedge (Overlap)

Make the corrections on the pattern first, then on the fabric. You may end up with pants that fit, without knowing how you did it, if you fail to readjust the pattern as you go along. Keeping track of everything now will result in a pattern that matches the final fit of the test pants. Remember, the goal is to have a *master pattern* with which you can sew the fit you want every time you make a pair of pants.

READJUSTING THE PATTERN

Make the changes on the pattern following the instructions that were given for making the initial pattern adjustments. These are explained in the section, ADJUSTING THE PATTERN. Added information about darts and curves not described previously is found in the section on *Extra Special Adjustments*.

The first pattern, on which you made all the initial adjustments, should be retained as is, for reference. *Mark the corrections on the pattern that you used to cut out your test pants.* Use pencil of contrasting color, such as red, for all changes. *Cross out the lines that no longer apply.* If you make a second correction, use a second color, such as blue, for clarity.

RE-FITTING THE PANTS

After you have completed the corrections on the pattern, make the same corrections on the pants. *Do not rip any more than you have to.* Mark the changes directly on the fabric with pencil, just as you did on the pattern, where a point is moved UP, DOWN, IN or OUT. Then redraw the stitching lines to the new point.

If possible, re-baste on the new stitching lines *before* ripping the original basting, as this minimizes shifting of the fabric grain.

Where the pattern is cut along the adjustment lines and spread or overlapped to change *crotch depth*, make the corresponding change on the pants by raising or lowering the entire waistline. Fold the casing or baste the waistband on at the new waistline position. Raise or lower the darts to correspond.

If there is not enough seam allowance to permit the amount of increase needed on the test pants, patch on a strip of fabric. Either make a tiny seam or join the strip on with fusible web, such as "Stitch Witchery", or fusible interfacing, such as "Easy Shaper, Light Weight".

If you do not wish to do this, there is another way to increase crotch depth on the pants, but it is hard to do it accurately. Stitch the crotch curve lower below the hipline, as shown here, then trim the seam.

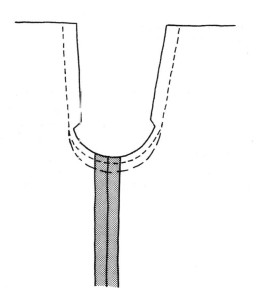

Where the pattern is cut along the wedge line and spread or overlapped to change the *wedge*, the side seams must be ripped from waist to hipline and the casing or waistband ripped from the waistline on the section to be changed. Lay the corrected pattern on the pants, matching hiplines, and match the *corrected* grainline of the pattern (from the hipline up) to the grainline you traced onto the fabric. Trace the new position of the side seam, waistline, and center line, using dressmakers' carbon of a different color than you used before. Baste together again on the new stitching lines, then rip the previous basting from the center seam. Now aren't you glad you made 1" seams?

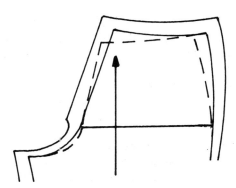

The broken line in the illustration shows the effect of decreasing the wedge. Notice that the center seamline is less bias when there is less wedge. Bias seams stretch and sag easily, as you know if you have ever made a bias-cut skirt. When the center seam is closer to straight grain, there is less stretch and less sag.

A little bias is desirable to allow some stretch on the crotch seam for ease in sitting and bending. Excessive bias due to excessive wedge contributes to sags under the seat.

EXTRA SPECIAL ADJUSTMENTS

You may require some further refinements not included in the previous instructions. Most of these involve changing the shape of the original pattern curves.

Crotch Curve

The crotch curve is the most difficult to draw and the most important to good fit. If you have *any* problems in this area you should check your pattern for *all* the special adjustments. Leaving any one of them to chance can complicate the problem because these adjustments are so inter-related.

The amount of wedge and the amount of crotch point extension both affect the depth of the curve that can be drawn at the crotch. One adjustment affects the next like a chain reaction. If any one is wrong it's like breaking one link of the chain.

The measurement of *waist indentation* is the clue to many problems. A small back waist indentation measurement indicates a flat seat. This requires less wedge, less crotch point extension, and a shorter diagonal on the crotch curve. A large back waist indentation indicates a prominent seat. This requires more wedge, more crotch point extension, and a longer diagonal. The comparison is shown here.

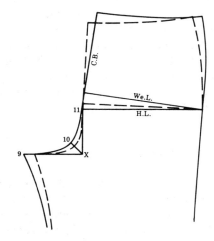

If the wedge is excessive, the angle of the center back seam limits the depth of the curve at the diagonal.

61

The wedge, the crotch point extension, and the diagonal should all be proportional and related to your figure shape and size. On basic pants, the *maximum* back crotch point extension is half the back pattern width at the hipline. The back *diagonal* is usually one-fourth the back crotch point extension.

The *maximum* front crotch point extension is one-fourth the front pattern width at hipline. Most figures deduct ¼" from this. A few deduct ½". The front *diagonal* is usually one half the front crotch point extension.

If your pants have fitting faults for which a change in crotch point extension is suggested, keep in mind these relationships. If very much of a change is made in hipline width, the crotch point extension and diagonal should be changed proportionally.

The *position* of the *back crotch curve* can have a tremendous effect on how the pants hang from there on down. If the crotch curve of the pants is higher than the body curve under the seat, the pants are bound to cut in or cling and pull wrinkles. The back crotch curve must be deep enough and low enough to allow the fabric to fall free from the seat. To lower the back crotch curve move Pt. 9 DOWN in back.

If your pants cling under the seat, first be sure the *crotch depth* is adequate. Then, if you have already adjusted Pt. 9 to make the back upper inseam ½" shorter than the front upper inseam (Pt. 8 to Pt. 9), try marking Pt. 9 DOWN another ¼". Draw a new crotchline as far as the centerline. Mark a new diagonal point (Pt. 10), then redraw the crotch curve.

It is probably easier to draw this change directly on the pants with colored pencil than to try to trace it from the pattern. You will have to rip the inseam from crotch to knee in order to join the front crotch point to the new back crotch point. You will have to stretch the back a little more as you join it to the front inseam.

Waistline Curve

The waistline of the pattern may be too straight for your figure. If you have a hollow where most people have a bulge, the pants may sag below the hollow. A change in the curve of the waistline often solves the problem. This may apply to the front, the back, or both. It may apply to one side only, if your figure is unevenly padded.

Redraw the waistline curve so it dips 1/8" to 3/8" lower at a point 4" from the center seam.

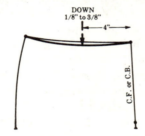

If your pattern has darts, fold in the darts on the pattern and redraw the waistline *over* the folded darts.

Dart Shape

Waistline darts may be either straight or curved. The shape should follow the shape of the body.

The seat dart should end 1" to 1½" above the hipline. A single dart in back may be either straight or slightly curved. If there are two darts in back, the center dart is straight. The side dart is usually shorter and may be either straight or curved. If you are rounded just below the waist in back, the side dart should be curved and shortened to 3" or 4" in length.

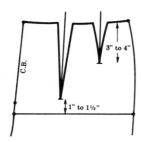

If you have a *flat* tummy, the front darts may be straight. A single dart may be about 4½" long. If there are two darts they are shorter. Most people need at least a little curve on the front darts for a becoming fit.

If you have a rounded tummy, the front darts should be curved and shortened to 3" in length. This releases more fabric to provide ease over the bulge. Redraw the stitching lines to curve inward 1/16" to 1/8" at a point halfway between waist and dart tip.

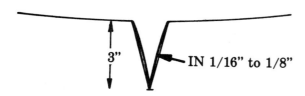

The measurement of *waist indentation* can help you understand how to adjust the width of the darts. Most people have a greater waist indentation in back than in front, therefore, the back darts are wider than the front darts on most patterns.

If your waist indentation is more in front and less in back, it indicates a rounded tummy and flat seat. You need wider darts in front and narrower darts in back.

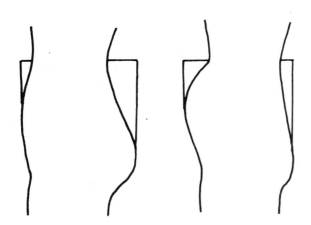

Added Darts

A single large dart will not fit as well as two smaller ones. If your figure is quite rounded below the waist or if you have prominent hip bones, add a dart if your pattern has only one. You will probably need to make the side dart wider than the center dart to fit over the prominent hip bone.

Make the new dart halfway between the original dart and the side seam. If this looks crowded, re-space the darts, adding more width at Pt. 2, if necessary. Start the center dart about one-third of the way between the center seam and side seam. Make the foldline parallel to the original dart, *not* parallel to the center seamline. All waistline darts are more becoming if slanted outward slightly. Re-shape the waistline curve over the folded darts.

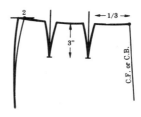

When pants with elastic have excessive gathers for a small waist, draw a dart halfway between center and side seam. Make it about ½" wide at the waistline, tapering to a point 3" below the waist. Extend parallel stitching lines through the casing.

If the excess fullness is only in the back, make the darts only in back. If there is also too much fullness in front, make darts in front also. If the resulting waistline is too tight to pull on over the hips, add a zipper. Pants fitted with darts and a waist-band are more suitable for figures with a slender waist.

Side Seam Shape

Sometimes the pants bulge out from the body at the side seams even though the circumference is correct. This happens when the side seam curve does not follow the shape of the body curve. The original pattern may have been too curved for your body, or an excessive curve may have resulted from an awkward adjustment, or from a sewing error.

Observe the shape of the seamline on the pattern and on the fabric. Where the bulge occurs, redraw a straighter line. This may be needed at the high hip, the hipline, or along the thigh. The seam should curve gently *outward* between the waist and hipline. It should curve slightly *inward* between the crotch and kneeline. Make the same correction on front and back patterns. The side seamlines should match.

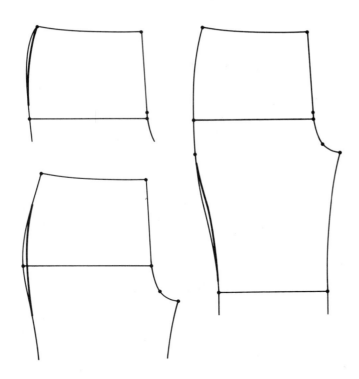

After extending the pantleg width at Pt. 7 and Pt. 8, as indicated in the section on "Fitting Faults", you may redraw the inseam from Pt. 8 to Pt. 9 with a straighter line than the original, to accommodate full thighs. Less curve on the inseam provides more ease over the inner thighs.

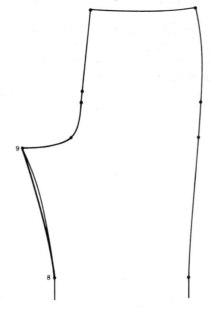

Inseam Shape

If the angle of the inseam is too great, the inseams will be too far apart at the knees for a figure with a close stance, knock knees, or thighs that touch. The pants may look fine on the hanger, but on the body the pantlegs pull in and cling against the inner thighs. This is what I call "bow-legged pants on a knock-kneed figure".

A figure with thin thighs, a wide stance, or bowlegs may wear pantlegs with more curve on the inseam if a close fit or narrow leg style is desired. The closer the fit, the more the leg shape is emphasized.

ADJUSTING TO YOUR PREFERENCE

When you have eliminated the fitting faults and have established the essential pattern requirements for well fitting basic pants, you may find you would still like to make a few changes to suit your preference. You may like a snugger fit or pantlegs that are wider or narrower than your pattern has provided. Suggestions are given in the section on Style that will help you achieve what you want.

COMPLETING THE TEST PANTS

When you are satisfied with the fit of the test pants, stitch seams and darts permanently, with matching thread. Excess seam allowance may be trimmed to 5/8".

Double stitch crotch seam or use a stretch stitch for durability. Clip seam allowance to seamline at center front and center back hip points. Press seam open above clips. Below the clips, the crotch seam may now be trimmed to ¼" and overcast.

Trim excess fabric from edge of casing. If fabric ravels, turn under raw edge and stitch in place. Fabrics that do not ravel should not be turned under as this creates unnecessary bulk. Machine-stitch overlapped ends of elastic. Insert zipper and complete waistband, following pattern instructions.

Turn under raw edges of hems or finish with flexible lace seam binding. Sew in place with a blind stitch. Set the creases by pressing with a wet press cloth. Hang on a hanger from the hems.

Making the Master Pattern

Check the accuracy of the final pattern by using it to make another pair of pants out of new fabric. Use the same type of fabric as you did before. If all the corrections were accurately made on the pattern as well as on the test pants, the new pants should fit the same way as the completed test pants.

A DURABLE PATTERN

You can make a durable copy of your final pattern by tracing it onto non-woven interfacing fabric. Use a non-stretching type, such as regular weight "Pellon", "Interlon", or "Shape-Aid".

Place the interfacing on top of the final pattern and pin together to prevent slipping. The interfacing should be transparent enough that you can see the pattern lines through it. Trace all stitching lines, fold lines, and grainlines with a fine felt-tip pen. Use a ruler to trace straight lines accurately. Include your hipline, kneeline, and front crotch line. Mark Pt. 4 on the back, the same distance below Pt. 3 as on the front.

Draw cutting lines, allowing 5/8" for seam allowance and 2" for hems. For the casing, allow 1½" if you like 1" elastic, or 1¼" for ¾" elastic. This provides for turning under ¼" along the raw edge. The waistband may be made any width you like.

Record the date on the pattern and indicate whether it is for knit or woven fabric.

Converting From Woven to Knit Fabric

If your pattern was fitted using woven fabric which has little "give", a change must be made for knit fabrics that stretch, such as doubleknit and jersey.

One inch of ease may be removed from the total circumference by decreasing the width ¼" on each side seam. Do this by moving Pt. 2, 3, 4, 5, and 6 IN ¼". Redraw the side seamlines and draw a new waistline to the adjusted side waist point.

If you wish, mark the seamlines for knit fabric on the same pattern you made for woven fabric. Use a contrast color for the lines that apply to knits, and label accordingly. You can use the same cutting lines for both types of fabric. The excess seam allowance may be trimmed from the knit fabric after stitching.

Converting From Knit Fabric to Woven

If your pattern was fitted using knit fabric that stretches, a change must be made for woven fabrics that don't stretch.

One inch of ease must be added to the total circumference by increasing the width ¼" on each side seam. Do this by moving Pt. 2, 3, 4, 5, and 6 OUT ¼". Redraw the side seamlines and draw a new waistline to the adjusted side waist point.

If you mark the seamlines for woven fabric on the same pattern you made for knits, you will have to mark new cutting lines to provide 5/8" seam allowance for the woven fabric. Be sure to use a contrast color for the lines that apply to woven fabric, and label accordingly.

THE TAGBOARD PATTERN

It is desirable to have a copy of your pattern made out of tagboard *without* seam allowance, for use in applying your fit to other patterns of various styles. Make one for knits and one for wovens. Instructions for using the tagboard pattern are given in the section on "SEWING WITH STYLE".

Tagboard may be purchased at a stationery or art supply store. You will need two pieces approximately 22" X 28" for each pattern.

Place your pattern on top of the tagboard, with carbon paper face down, in between. Carefully trace all stitching lines from waist to knee. Trace the hipline and wedge line. Draw the grainline from the knee to the crotchline. Make a hole at the top of the grainline, just large enough for a pencil point, and another near the bottom.

Cut out the tagboard pattern *on* the seamlines and along the waistline and kneeline. Cut a notch at Pt. 3, Pt. 4, Pt. 11, and Pt. 12. Measure the distance from knee to hemline on your master pattern and record on the tagboard pattern. Label with the date and whether it is for woven or knit fabric.

Sewing With Style

USING THE MASTER PATTERN

Now you can apply your fit to a variety of fashions using your master pattern. The durable copies of your basic pattern may be used again and again whenever you make basic pants. The tagboard patterns may be used to pre-fit commercial style patterns, or as a basis for developing your own style variations.

If you like to wear jeans or other styles fitted more snugly than the basic master pattern, follow the directions for jeans. Make a durable copy with seam allowance for repeated use and make a tagboard copy without seam allowance to use for style development. Label the jeans pattern and note the type of fabric to be used.

Whether you pre-fit a commercial style pattern or make your own, be sure to use the appropriate tagboard for the type of fabric you intend to use. Every time you make a new style, label the pattern and attach a sample of the fabric used to help you identify it in the future.

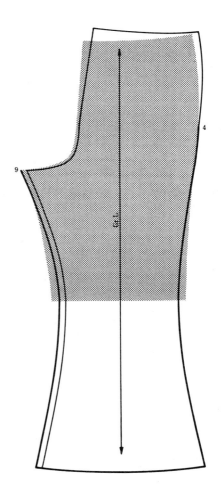

Pre-Fitting Commercial Style Patterns

It is easy to use the leg style of a commercial pattern with the fitting lines of your master pattern for the upper part.

Draw the crotchline on the *front* of the commercial pattern. Label Pt. 4. Mark the position of Pt. 4 on the back pattern, the same distance below the waist as on the front. Place the appropriate tagboard pattern on top of the corresponding commercial pattern pieces, matching at Pt. 4, with grainlines parallel. Trace the outline of your tagboard onto the commercial pattern from Pt. 4 upward, and around to Pt. 9.

Use the style lines of the commercial pattern from crotchline to hemline. If your crotch point does not coincide with that of the commercial pattern, draw the inseam from your personal Pt. 9 to the hem, parallel to that of the style pattern. Lengthen or shorten at the hem, as needed.

Jeans

Jeans are intended to fit more snugly than basic pants. They are suitable for small figures with a flat seat and a flat tummy. They are not recommended for the larger figure with rounded contours. Typically, jeans are worn skin tight, or close to it, but you can vary the degree of snugness to suit yourself. After you adjust the fit to your taste, apply the style details of your choice.

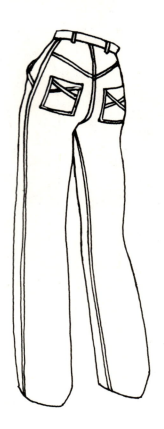

Make a working copy of your master pattern with darts, by tracing around your tagboard. Mark the grainline position through the holes and connect with a straight line. Extend straight lines from knee to hem, the amount indicated on your tagboard, plus ½".

Draw the changes in red. Decrease the width at the side seams on front and back, as follows:

Mark IN ¼" from Pt. 2, 3, and 4. Mark IN ¾" from Pt. 5 and 6. Match the tagboard to the marks at Pt. 2 and 4 and trace the outline between these points. Match at Pt. 4 and 5 and trace. Draw a straight line from Pt. 5 to Pt. 6.

Decrease the width at the inseams as follows:

Back: Mark IN ½" at Pt. 7, 8, and 9. Draw a straight line from Pt. 7 to Pt. 8. Trace the inseam from Pt. 8 to Pt. 9 along the edge of the tagboard.

Front: Mark IN ½" at Pt. 7 and 8. Connect with a straight line. Trace the inseam from Pt. 8 to Pt. 9 along the edge of the tagboard.

If desired, increase the curve on the inseams of front and back for a tighter fit on the thighs.

Decrease the front wedge ¼". *Increase* the back wedge ½". It is essential to have a bigger wedge in back on tightly fitted pants, or you may not be able to sit down!

Decrease the crotch depth ¼" for a still tighter fit. Add seam allowance and hem allowance and label appropriately.

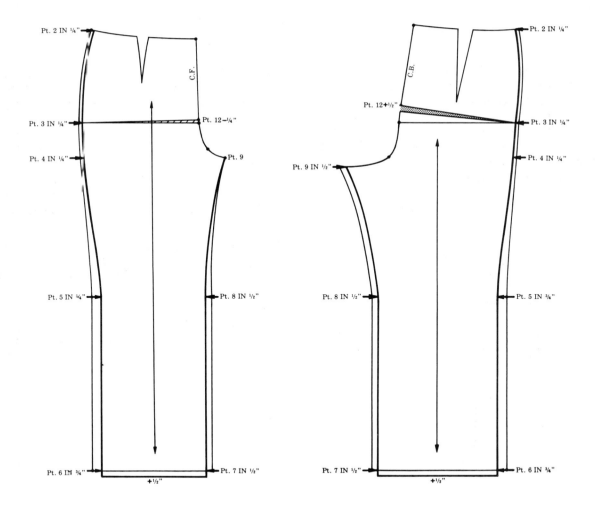

Style details for jeans usually include belt loops on the waistband, a yoke and patch pockets in back, a fly-front zipper, and cut-in pockets in front. Use a big stitch for double rows of top-stitching to accent edges.

Making Your Own Style Patterns

It's fun to carry out your own ideas in styling and it is easier than you may imagine. Many different effects can be achieved by simple changes of length, width, shaping, and details. Suggestions are given here for making your own patterns for many popular styles, starting with your master pattern. The joy of it is, you know your creation will fit your figure.

For each style you wish to make, start with the appropriate tagboard pattern. Trace a working copy, including grainlines, then make the style changes in red. Add seam allowance, hems, and labels.

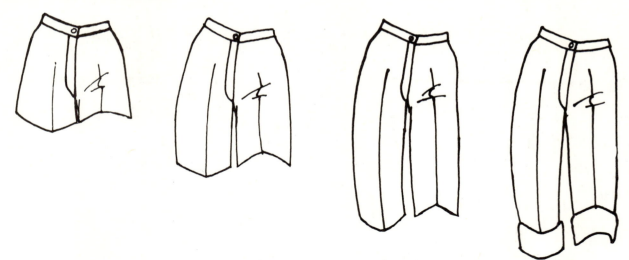

Typical lengths of popular styles are shown in the illustration. For *below-the-knee* variations, simply mark the desired length below the knee and draw a new hemline parallel to the kneeline, the same on front and back.

For *above-the-knee* lengths, mark the desired length at the side seams. Draw a straight line at right angles to the grainline from this mark to the inseam on front and back. Add ¼" length to the front pattern at inseam. Connect to the straight line with a slight curve, as shown.

Measure the front inseam from Pt. 9 to the new hemline. On the back, measure down from Pt. 9 and mark the same inseam length. Connect with a curve to the straight line.

Increase or decrease the width at the hemline as desired for a looser or closer fit around the leg. You may make this change at the side seam, inseam, or both.

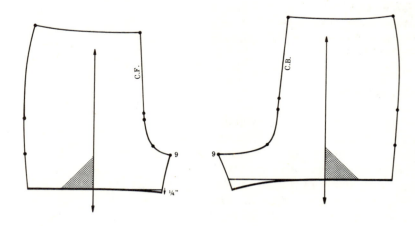

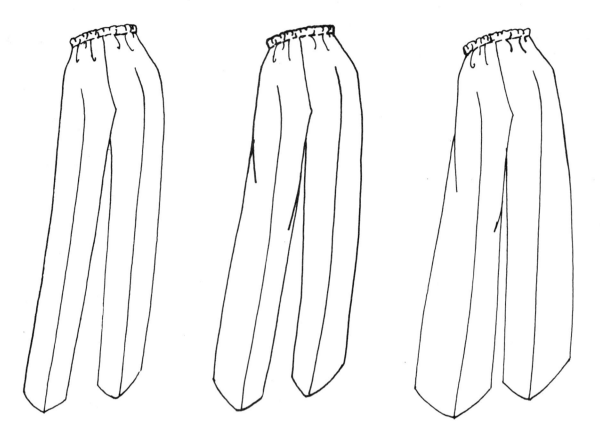

Straight pantlegs may be narrow, wide, or any width in between. Make minor changes in width on the side seam. For very *narrow* pantlegs, decrease the width at the inseam also. The smallest pantleg circumference you can use is approximately equal to your knee circumference plus 2", in straight pantlegs.

For *wide, straight pantlegs*, draw the side seams parallel to the grainline from hipline to hemline. These may be made without a side seam if you wish. Join the front and back patterns, matching side seams from Pt. 3 to Pt. 6. Cross out the seam below Pt. 3. Convert the seamlines to a dart above Pt. 3.

For no-side-seam pants with a drawstring or elastic waistline, eliminate the entire side seam and extend the waistline by connecting Pt. 2 front to Pt. 2 back.

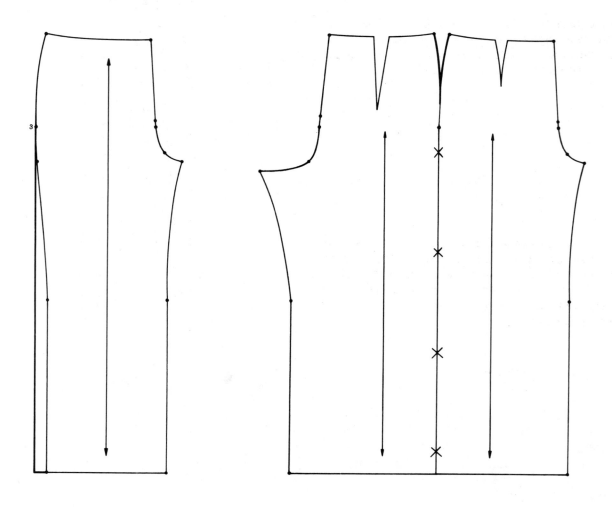

Tapered pantlegs are narrower at the hem than at the knee. For moderate taper, mark IN ½" to 1" at Pt. 6 and Pt. 7. Redraw side seamlines to the knee. For narrow tapered pants, mark IN at Pt. 5 and Pt. 8 also.

Measure your foot around the instep to determine the smallest pantleg circumference you can wear. If you want pants narrower than this you can put a zipper in the side seams at the ankle.

Flared pantlegs are wider at the hem than at the knee. You can create various effects depending on the amount of width added and where the flare begins. Add width in equal amounts at Pt. 6 and Pt. 7 to keep the fullness balanced. Add the same to front and back.

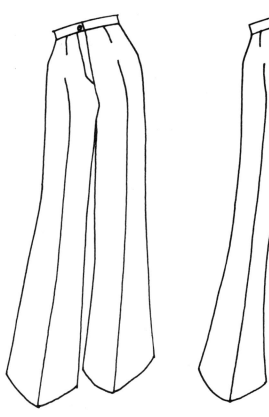

For *moderately flared basic pants,* mark the flare points at the knee, Pt. 5 and Pt. 8. Add ¼" to 1" width at Pt. 6 and Pt. 7. Redraw seamlines straight from knee to hem.

For *moderately flared hostess pants,* use a copy of your wide, straight-leg pants, with side seams parallel to the grainline. Mark high hip point on side seamline 3" below Pt. 2. Mark 1" to 4" additional width at Pt. 6. Connect a straight line from this mark to the high hip point.

Measure from Pt. 2 downward and mark the side seam length at hem, the same length as on the wide, straight-leg pants. Extend the hemline in a slight curve to meet the side seam.

Draw the inseam straight from Pt. 9 to Pt. 7, parallel to the grainline. Fold the pattern in half, bringing Pt. 6 and Pt. 7 together and crease. Draw a new grainline along the crease. Cross out the original grainline. Use a soft fabric, such as jersey or crepe. *Do not press* creases into soft pants.

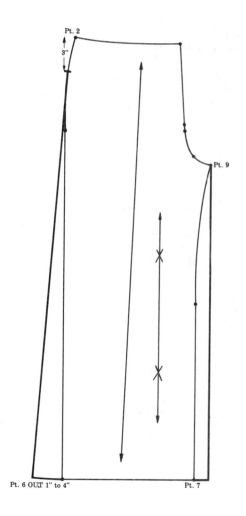

The flare is *accentuated* when the pantlegs are fitted closer above the flare point. To do this, decrease the width ½" to 1" at Pt. 5 and Pt. 8. Redraw to Pt. 4 and Pt. 9.

Increase the width 1" to 2" at Pt. 6 and Pt. 7. Connect with a slightly curved line from knee to hem. Measure from the new position of Pt. 5 toward the hem and mark the side seam length from Pt. 5 to Pt. 6, the same as on the master pattern. Mark the inseam length the same, from Pt. 8 to Pt. 7. Extend the hemline in a slight curve to meet at Pt. 6 and Pt. 7.

Culottes are pants with enough fullness added to resemble a skirt. Use a copy of your wide, straight-leg pattern. Increase crotch depth ¼" to ½". Remove all of the front wedge. Reduce the back wedge to ¼". Extend the back width at Pt. 9 by 1" plus the amount you reduced the back wedge. Draw the centerline on the front pattern from Pt. 11 to the crotchline and label Pt. X. Extend the front width at Pt. 9, making the distance from Pt. X to the crotch point equal to half the front pattern width at hipline, minus 1". Redraw the front crotch curve, increasing the diagonal ¼".

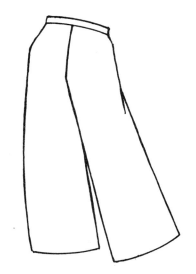

Mark length desired and draw new hemline. Add ½" to 2" extra width at Pt. 6. Draw side seamlines straight from Pt. 6, blending in to the curve at hip. Draw inseams from Pt. 9 to hemline, parallel to the grainline. Complete the hemlines following directions given for hostess pants.

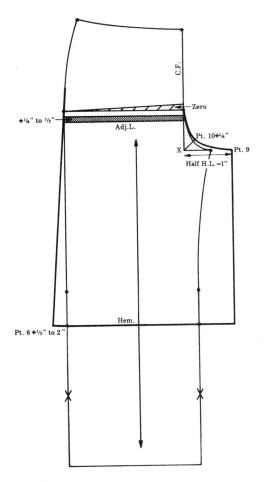

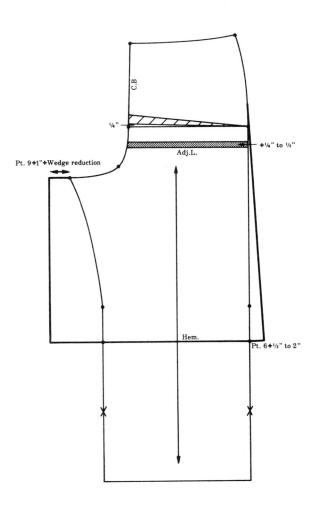

Hip yokes may be used in front, in back, or both. Use your master pattern with darts. Fold together the darts, matching stitching lines and tape in place. Draw the yoke line in the desired shape over the folded darts. Mark notches, as shown, then cut off the yoke section.

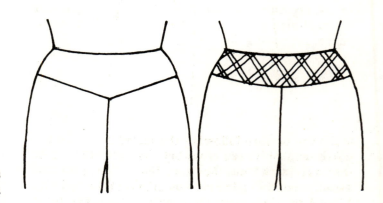

A *faced waistline* provides a smooth finish for pants with darts. To make the facing pattern, trace a copy of your master pattern from waistline to high hip. Cut through each dart and overlap, bringing stitching lines together. Tape in place. Draw the lower edge of the facing across the closed darts, 2½" below the waistline. Reduce the ease on the facing pieces by redrawing the side seamlines IN ¼".

Add seam allowance along the waistline, side seams, and along the center seam next to the zipper opening. Mark the other center line "Place on fold". Mark grainlines parallel to center lines. Label front and back.

Untape any part of a dart that extends below the yoke line and cross it out. The resulting fullness is eased along the yoke seam. Label accordingly. Indicate which center line is to be placed on the fold. Add seam allowance to all other edges.

Mark grainlines parallel to the center lines, unless you would like a bias yoke. In that case, draw the grainline at a 45 degree angle to the center lines. Since bias stretches very easily, trim ¼" off the side seams of the bias yoke pattern.

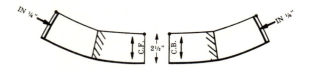

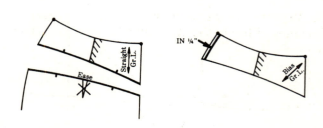

When you make the pants, sew a stay into the waistline to prevent stretching. You can use a piece of straight seam binding, cut the length of your waist measure, A-7. Baste this to the wrong side of the pants along the waistline, easing the fabric to fit the binding. This is joined into the seam when you sew on the facing.

Make patterns for the yoke facing the same as the yoke, except trim ¼" off each side seam. Don't forget appropriate labels for each pattern piece.

A *contour waistband* is curved to fit the body curve below the waist. It is joined to the pants below the natural waistline. The top of the band usually rests at the natural waist. The width is about 1" to 1½".

Make the pattern following the instructions for hip yokes, except do not cross out the part of the dart that extends below the yoke line. Decrease the ease by redrawing the side seamlines of the band IN ¼". Add 1" or more for overlap where the band meets the zipper opening. Be sure to interface a contour band. Fusible interfacing is recommended for this.

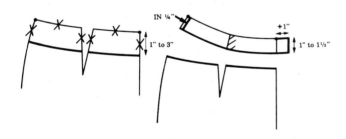

Hip huggers are pants with a lowered waistline. They may either be faced or finished with a contour band.

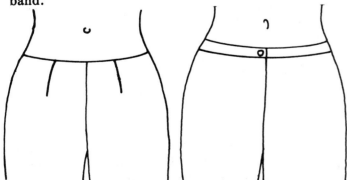

Use the master pattern with darts. Draw the lowered waistline where you want the finished edge to be. This is usually 1" to 3" below the natural waist. For a faced top, add seam allowance, then trim away and discard the excess part of the pattern. Make a facing pattern to fit the lowered waistline, as described previously.

If you want a contour band, draw another line an even distance below the finished waistline. The amount of the additional lowering is equal to the width of the band. Add seam allowance, then trim off the excess part of the pattern. If the remainder of the dart on the main pattern piece is 3/8" wide or less at the top, cross out the stitching lines and ease the fullness at the seam. Otherwise, stitch the remainder of the dart.

Added Seams

Seams may be added to create design lines for special effects. Some western style pants have a *chevron-shaped* seam at the knee. Draw the design line across the pantleg. Cut apart and add seam allowance to each edge.

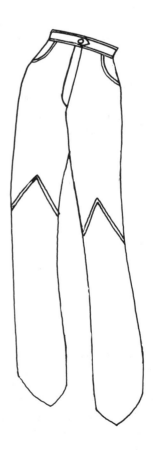

Vertical seams may be added at front or back. Extend the crease line to the waist. The dart point should end on the crease line. If necessary, move the dart over. If there are two darts, the center dart should be in line with the crease line. The side dart should be half-way between the crease line and side seam.

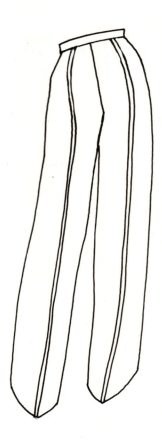

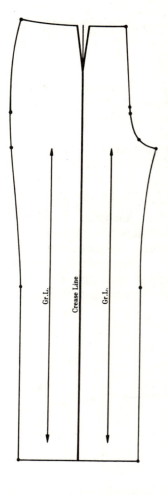

It is possible to curve a vertical seam into a contour seam. For this and other more complicated styles utilize a commercial pattern.

Cut the pattern apart along the crease line to the dart, then along the dart lines to the waist. Leave the side dart intact. Draw a grainline on each pattern piece, parallel to the crease line.

Add seam allowance to each edge. You may topstitch the seam for emphasis. This is especially suitable on "Ultrasuede" and on any fabric you cannot crease.

Your fashion future

Many fashion details are easily adapted to your master pattern. You can learn a lot by comparing a commercial style pattern to a basic pattern of the same size. Place the style pattern on top of the basic pattern, matching crotchlines, with grainlines parallel. Measure the differences at each pattern point.

Consult books on pattern drafting to learn more about how style patterns are made. "Flat pattern" methods are fun to learn and easy to apply.

Observe the style details of ready-to-wear for ideas. Experiment, enjoy yourself, and keep growing. Share what you learn with others. May your efforts be rewarded with the joy of pride and confidence every time you sew *pants fit for your figure*.

Appendix

CHECK-LIST OF TOOLS AND SUPPLIES

For Taking Body Measurements

Tape measure, 60" non-stretch fiberglass
Yardstick
Dressmaker's gauge
Board, 9" X 12" plywood or masonite
Narrow belt
1/8" elastic

For Adjusting The Pattern

Basic pants pattern
Freezer paper, plastic coated
Ruler, clear plastic, preferrably "C-THRU B-85"
Triangle or L-square, 12" X 12"
#2 lead pencil
Colored pencils, blue and red, erasable
Pattern paper
Transparent tape, "Magic" type
Plastic "oilcloth", 2/3 yd. of 54" width
Scissors
Pins

For Making Test Pants

Fabric, broadcloth or doubleknit
Casing elastic or zipper
Graphite paper or dressmaker's carbon
Tracing wheel, smooth edge
Cotton basting thread

For Making Master Patterns

Non-woven interfacing, non-stretching
Tagboard

TABLE OF DIVISIONS

Amounts	Divided by 2	Amounts	Divided by 2	Amounts	Divided by 2
1/4	1/8	6-1/2	3-1/4	18-1/2	9-1/4
1/2	1/4	7	3-1/2	19	9-1/2
3/4	3/8	7-1/2	3-3/4	19-1/2	9-3/4
1	1/2	8	4	20	10
1-1/4	5/8	8-1/2	4-1/4	20-1/2	10-1/4
1-1/2	3/4	9	4-1/2	21	10-1/2
1-3/4	7/8	9-1/2	4-3/4	21-1/2	10-3/4
2	1	10	5	22	11
2-1/4	1-1/8	10-1/2	5-1/4	22-1/2	11-1/4
2-1/2	1-1/4	11	5-1/2	23	11-1/2
2-3/4	1-3/8	11-1/2	5-3/4	23-1/2	11-3/4
3	1-1/2	12	6	24	12
3-1/4	1-5/8	12-1/2	6-1/4	24-1/2	12-1/4
3-1/2	1-3/4	13	6-1/2	25	12-1/2
3-3/4	1-7/8	13-1/2	6-3/4	25-1/2	12-3/4
4	2	14	7	26	13
4-1/4	2-1/8	14-1/2	7-1/4	26-1/2	13-1/4
4-1/2	2-1/4	15	7-1/2	27	13-1/2
4-3/4	2-3/8	15-1/2	7-3/4	27-1/2	13-3/4
5	2-1/2	16	8	28	14
5-1/4	2-5/8	16-1/2	8-1/4	28-1/2	14-1/4
5-1/2	2-3/4	17	8-1/2	29	14-1/2
5-3/4	2-7/8	17-1/2	8-3/4	29-1/2	14-3/4
6	3	18	9	30	15

Amounts	Divided by 2	Amounts	Divided by 2	Amounts	Divided by 4
30-1/2	15-1/4	43	21-1/2	4	1
31	15-1/2	43-1/2	21-3/4	4-1/4	1-1/16
31-1/2	15-3/4	44	22	4-1/2	1-1/8
32	16	44-1/2	22-1/4	4-3/4	1-3/16
32-1/2	16-1/4	45	22-1/2	5	1-1/4
33	16-1/2	45-1/2	22-3/4	5-1/4	1-5/16
33-1/2	16-3/4	46	23	5-1/2	1-3/8
34	17	46-1/2	23-1/4	5-3/4	1-7/16
34-1/2	17-1/4	47	23-1/2	6	1-1/2
35	17-1/2	47-1/2	23-3/4	6-1/4	1-9/16
35-1/2	17-3/4	48	24	6-1/2	1-5/8
36	18	48-1/2	24-1/4	6-3/4	1-11/16
36-1/2	18-1/4	49	24-1/2	7	1-3/4
37	18-1/2	49-1/2	24-3/4	7-1/4	1-13/16
37-1/2	18-3/4	50	25	7-1/2	1-7/8
38	19	50-1/2	25-1/4	7-3/4	1-15/16
38-1/2	19-1/4	51	25-1/2	8	2
39	19-1/2	51-1/2	25-3/4		
39-1/2	19-3/4	52	26		
40	20	52-1/2	26-1/4		
40-1/2	20-1/4	53	26-1/2		
41	20-1/2	53-1/2	26-3/4		
41-1/2	20-3/4	54	27		
42	21	54-1/2	27-1/4		
42-1/2	21-1/4	55	27-1/2		

TABLE OF METRIC EQUIVALENTS

This chart gives the standard equivalents as approved by the pattern fashion industry.

CONVERTING INCHES INTO MILLIMETERS AND CENTIMETERS

(SLIGHTLY ROUNDED FOR YOUR CONVENIENCE)

inches	mm		cm	inches	cm	inches	cm
⅛	3mm			7	18	29	73.5
¼	6mm			8	20.5	30	76
⅜	10mm	or	1cm	9	23	31	78.5
½	13mm	or	1.3cm	10	25.5	32	81.5
⅝	15mm	or	1.5cm	11	28	33	84
¾	20mm	or	2cm	12	30.5	34	86.5
⅞	22mm	or	2.2cm	13	33	35	89
1	25mm	or	2.5cm	14	35.5	36	91.5
				15	38	37	94
1¼	32mm	or	3.2cm	16	40.5	38	96.5
1½	38mm	or	3.8cm	17	43	39	99
1¾	45mm	or	4.5cm	18	46	40	102
2	50mm	or	5cm	19	48.5	41	104
2½	65mm	or	6.3cm	20	51	42	107
3	75mm	or	7.5cm	21	53.5	43	109
3½	90mm	or	9cm	22	56	44	112
4	100mm	or	10cm	23	58.5	45	115
				24	61	46	117
4½	115mm	or	11.5cm	25	63.5	47	120
5	125mm	or	12.5cm	26	66	48	122
5½	140mm	or	14cm	27	68.5	49	125
6	150mm	or	15cm	28	71	50	127

INDEX OF ADJUSTMENTS

Additional copies of PANTS FIT FOR YOUR
FIGURE may be ordered by sending a check or
money order to:

Vista Publications
3010 Santa Monica Blvd. Suite 221-B
Santa Monica, CA 90404

Price: $9.95 plus 75¢ for postage and handling.
California residents please add 48¢ sales tax.